THE 1984
VERITY BARGATE AWARD
SHORT PLAYS

edited by
BARRIE KEEFFE

UP FOR NONE
by Mick Mahoney

COMING APART
by Melissa Murray

A Methuen New Theatrescript
Methuen · London and New York

the 1983 Verity Bargate Award-winning Plays

SHONA, LUNCH GIRLS, THE SHELTER
by Tony Craze, Ron Hart, Johnnie Quarrell

A METHUEN PAPERBACK

First published in Great Britain in 1985 as a Methuen Paperback original by Methuen London Ltd, 11 New Fetter Lane, London EC4P 4EE and in the United States of America by Methuen Inc, 733 Third Avenue, New York, NY 10017

British Library Cataloguing in Publication Data

Mahoney, Mick
    Up for none; and, Coming apart. — (A Methuen
    new theatrescript)
    1. English drama — 20th century
    I. Title   II. Murray, Melissa. Coming apart
    822'.914'08   PR1272

    ISBN 0-413-58930-7

CAUTION
All rights in these plays are reserved. Applications for permission to perform them in whole or in part must be made in advance, before rehearsals begin, to the authors' respective agents, as follows:
Mick Mahoney: Rochelle Stevens & Co, 64 Prebend Street, Islington, London N1 8PS
Melissa Murray: Michael Imison Playwrights Ltd, 28 Almeida Street, London N1

Set in IBM 10 point Press Roman by
Words & Pictures Ltd, Thornton Heath, Surrey
Printed in Great Britain by
Redwood Burn Ltd., Trowbridge, Wiltshire.

The Verity Bargate Award

In 1969 Verity Bargate and Fred Proud set up the Soho Theatre Company in Soho. It moved to its present location in Riding House Street in 1971 where it became the Soho Poly Theatre. From this base Verity gave the first helping hand to hundreds of new writers by premiering their work. She gained the theatre an international reputation for her work with new and developing writers and the one act play. Some of the writers whose early work she premiered were: Howard Brenton, Pam Gems, Gilly Fraser, Brian Clarke, Tony Marchant, and myself.

This award was established to commemorate the remarkable contribution made by a woman of extraordinary instinct and drive in the field of new writing, and to carry on her work by the continuing encouragement of new playwrights.

Eligibility
The only restrictions on entries were that they should be new, unperformed plays and that they should be suitable for production at a small theatre such as the Soho Poly. The award comprises a cash prize and publication by Methuen London Ltd.

Selection
The members of the Verity Bargate Award Committee and the Fund Raising Committee gathered to read all the entries and, in consultation, drew up a shortlist of twelve plays, from which the judges made the final selection. All plays were given the same consideration regardless of style, content and form; quality and potential were the only guidelines.

Judges
The judges for the 1984 award chaired by Nick Hern, drama editor of Methuen London, were: Irving Wardle, drama critic of *The Times*; Richard Eyre, director; Maggie Steed, actress; Tony Craze, last year's winner and the Soho Poly's writer-in-residence; and Sue Dunderdale, Artistic Director of the Soho Poly.

Barrie Keeffe

Contents

UP FOR NONE

Characters

SNEAKY
RUCKER
BRASS
CAT
P.C. YOUNG

Scene One

The set is Oxford Street; an empty shop doorway. In it stands a young man of sixteen or so years of age. He has shortish hair, a side parting, wears an expensive tracksuit top, faded straight-leg jeans cut straight at the bottom and cut at the seam for an inch or so – giving a small flare. He stands looking left, then right. After a minute or so he pulls out ten Embassy and lights one. Thirty seconds later another chap enters stage left. He wears a white T-shirt, Levi red tag jeans, English brogues and a worried expression. He is older and taller. He is carrying a large wooden case.

SNEAKY: Get some crates, eh?

RUCKER (*he has a bandaged right hand*): Yeah, all right. (*As he leaves the stage.*) Co's on.

SNEAKY (*pulling twenty Bensons from his back pocket*): That's all I need, co's. Trouble with the country. Too many cossers and not enough criminals. Police carrying guns and arresting fly-pitchers. (*He lights a cigarette.*) Mind you, could have a fiddle today. Plenty of weight up here. It's gone though, this street. Fucking whole game's gone. What you want is a sunbed shop. Don't stop taking readies. Where's he gone? Gotta be the worst outside man up here. Don't stop fighting the kid. Something wrong with his brain cell. That's who they wanna be nicking, pot-houses like that.

(*RUCKER re-enters carrying two milk-crates.*)

RUCKER: Could only find these.

SNEAKY: See you later, Rucker.

RUCKER: Yeah. All right. (*He goes.*)

SNEAKY: Lively roll call. (*Turning away from the audience.*) She doesn't stop weeding money. 'Bout time she got herself a job. Wants to buy herself a car now. Wonder how much that'll cost me. (*He mimics his girlfriend.*) Oh, it's really nice Sneaky, tinted windows, roll bars. She's only selling it 'cos Stevie's got her a Golf. (*He resumes his normal voice.*) It had better stop those fucking headaches. Most birds need Anadin, mine needs a Mini.

A few years ago it was bang-on up here of a Saturday. Go and get yourself a lively monkey. Well, you'd get something worst ways. All you get now is nicked. It's down to all those slags Oxford Street Trading Association. Talk about big eyes, greedy cunts, straight. That Mr Selfridge must be on the handbone all day long, 'They're still outside Sergeant.' (*He shuts up as he watches someone walk past.*) Got packets, them Arabs, fucking bundles! Blinding geezer, him, God. 'I'll give you plenty of readies. You can have wealth beyond your dreams, but you've gotta be an Arab.' (*He watches an imaginary Arab.*) Have a look, straight into Marks and Spencers – ten of everything, same colour, same size, dresses, shoes, bras, knickers. He's happy. The harem's happy. Everybody's fucking happy. Where's he got to with them crates? Those kids out of Edgware Road, they're all double slow.

Come on Rucker. It's bang-on here. I suppose he's got caught up somewhere having a chat about steel toe-caps. He had the right idea, Prince Charles. Shove 'em in the army.

(*RUCKER enters carrying a milk crate.*)

Where've you been?

RUCKER: All over the place. I had to chin somebody for this.

SNEAKY: Yeah. All right.

RUCKER: He was only a Paki.

SNEAKY: Are you mad? There'll be fucking murders.

RUCKER: Not worried by a few Pakis are you?

SNEAKY: They'll scream the gaff down. (*With an Indian accent*.) It was a racist attack and if you don't find the man responsible we know it's because we are Indian. (*Normal voice again*.) They'll be nicking anyone near a fucking milk crate.

RUCKER: Bollocks. They don't care about Paks.

SNEAKY: What do you know?

RUCKER: Bit more than you it seems.

SNEAKY: Yeah. You're a right shrewd nut, Rucker. Stand them up. (*He indicates the crates*.) I wanna check the gear. (RUCKER *stacks crates*. SNEAKY *puts the case on top. He begins opening boxes*.) Suppose you'll go on from here to be a brain surgeon, eh?

RUCKER: No value, brain surgeon. Takes years and they're still on half wages when they've cracked it. No, I wanna line where you apply little effort and get maximum results. 'Murder Inc.' – they had the right idea.

SNEAKY: Yeah. All right. (*The case is slightly unstable*.) Hold the case Rucker.

RUCKER: Say, for instance, you wanted someone dead and then you said to me 'Kill him and I'll give you two grand', I then find his address and with a needle inject his milk with arsenic or cyanide. Simple, see.

SNEAKY: Say he doesn't have his milk delivered?

RUCKER: Letter bomb.

SNEAKY: Yeah, but that would probably kill his secretary.

RUCKER: There's a million ways of killing people.

SNEAKY: Go and get some coffee, eh?

RUCKER: Yeah. All right.

SNEAKY: I want a coffee, no sugar and a chicken salad sandwich with brown bread.

RUCKER (*receiving money*): Yeah. All right.

SNEAKY (*as RUCKER leaves*): Make sure it's brown bread.

RUCKER: Yeah. All right.

SNEAKY (*opening packages with increasing haste*): All black faced! Untold strokes those fuckin' wholesalers! It's a farce up here on Saturdays. Co's are on. Rucker's doing me brain in. Now I've got all black faces. That fat Sid. He's sat up all night sorting these out. (*He transports the audience to* SID's *ménage*.) 'Coming up Sidney?'

'Yes Miriam, just serving Sneaky the Yok.'

(*Himself again*.) Two-fifty these watches, madam. No, sorry I've only got those with the black face. (*He watches an imaginary customer walk away*.) Fucking Yossell. What a slag. The Yorkshire Ripper give him a ten black. I can't see me getting to eat with these fucking things. Should have gone to Aussie with Archie. Piss hole this gaff, I wanted to go horse riding up Child's Hill with her. Could stay in. Murder Saturday night, anyway. Silly Northerners singing football songs in Covent Garden. They're not that silly. Not too many singing down Mile End Road. How could you be a Northerner? I wouldn't be a Northerner for a million pounds a week. (*re-enter* RUCKER.)

That was quick. Mind you, they probably served you first, eh, being Italian. You being a mob man and all Rucker.

RUCKER: Nobody in there. Here 'are.

SNEAKY (*looking into a bag*): I can't believe you. I've had it so often, you've got to be winding me up.

RUCKER: What?

SNEAKY: One, I've got white bread. Two, without opening this coffee, I'll bet your wages this has got sugar in it.

RUCKER: Yeah. All right.

SNEAKY (*tasting the coffee*): Just lost your wages. No money today Rucker.

RUCKER: Yeah. All right.

SNEAKY: You agreed to the bet.

RUCKER: Yeah. All right.

SNEAKY: I said, I bet you your wages. You said 'Yeah. All right'.

RUCKER: Let's taste the coffee.

SNEAKY: There's sugar in it.

RUCKER: No there ain't.

SNEAKY: There is Rucker.

RUCKER: I can't taste it.

SNEAKY: I'll let you off this time.

RUCKER: Yeah. All right.

SNEAKY: Is that all they teach you in school?

RUCKER: What?

SNEAKY: Yeah — all right.

RUCKER: I don't go to school . . . I'm banned.

SNEAKY: What?

RUCKER: Banned. Go within a mile radius of the school and I'm nicked. Done me maths teacher with a chair.

SNEAKY: You're a fucking menace.

RUCKER: Kept picking on me.

SNEAKY: Do well with that attitude. What happened to the teacher?

RUCKER: She's in hospital.

(SNEAKY *casts his eyes to the skies.*)

SNEAKY: The Polar Bear's on Selfridges. I'm going to see if I can get any white faces off him. That slag Sid's given me all black. Don't really like asking Polar, the scouse cunt. That Sid's a fucking dog.

RUCKER: Give us a cockle. I'll give him a dig.

SNEAKY: Switch off. You want to slow down with all that bollocks. Making yourself a right mug. Chinning people for tenners.

RUCKER: Done a bubble last night. Got an apple.

SNEAKY: You might get a few apples, Rucker, but you'll get a few Mars Bars and all.

RUCKER: Few scars don't worry me.

SNEAKY: If you like blood, be a butcher. If you like fighting, be a boxer. Either way you'll get more readies and you'll live longer. Because the way you're going is one way and all the sis that go that way end up the same way — dead.

RUCKER: Yeah. All right.

SNEAKY: I don't need this. We ain't taken a dinar. Co's are on and my brain's done in. I am going down to see Polar. The watches are fifty bob. The bangles are a ching. Don't go any lower than that. We should be hand billing them at fivers. You can go two quids on them watches. You want this roll? — I can't eat white bread.

RUCKER *stands by the case which is placed on top of three milk crates. It is open and neatly laid out on top of some blue velvet are a variety of watches and some lighters, bangles etc. He stands silently — occasionally nodding to someone.*

At one point he drags the gear back into a shop doorway and watches a van pass; he then brings the case back on to the street.

RUCKER: The bangles madam. They're ten pounds. How much do you want to pay? Five. I'll tell you what, six pounds. Yes – how many, three? That's eighteen pounds before that policeman comes. Policeman – you know – Hello, Hello, Hello. You know. Dar – Dar – Dar – Dar. That's it, policeman. Yes, yes. Fucking Africans. *(He puts the money into the case, except for his three quid. He stands quietly for a minute or so and then there is another customer.*

Don't touch the gear. Oi, leave it alone. Yes, go on, fuck off. He weren't a bad judge that Idi Amin.

(A young woman walks on stage. She wears a black pencil skirt, red blouse which is slightly see-through, black bra, black seamed stockings and red high heels. She is about twenty-four or twenty-five. She has a northern accent.)

How's it going?

BRASS: Not bad. I want another one then I am going home.

RUCKER: Had one already?

BRASS: Two.

RUCKER: How much?

BRASS: Both forty. I've got to be home lively though. They're coming to lay the carpet today. Where's he gone?

RUCKER: To see if he can get some white-faced watches. He . . .

BRASS *at same point turns away from* RUCKER, *puffs out her chest and pouts her lips.*

BRASS *(to an imaginary customer)*: You want it? *(Pause.)* Go on, fuck off then.

RUCKER: Bit old ain't he?

BRASS: Spend twenty minutes wanking him off normally.

RUCKER: What if it won't go? . . .

BRASS: That's his problem.

RUCKER: Still get paid though?

BRASS: Yeah. You get the money first.

RUCKER: You enjoy your work?

BRASS: Not with a punter. I couldn't enjoy it with one of them.

RUCKER: Is it different then?

BRASS: 'Course it is.

RUCKER: You been down here long then?

BRASS: Three years. Used to just come down weekends.

RUCKER: Where you from?

BRASS: Leicester.

RUCKER: Leicester, that's all Pakis innit?

BRASS: Fucking Bangladesh. In Highfields the road signs are in fucking Asian.

RUCKER: Is that where you come from?

BRASS: Yeah.

RUCKER: That why you moved?

BRASS: Not really. It was bloody stupid. I kept getting a pasting every Sunday night. He kept saying I was hiding the money, so one week I missed the 7.05 Inter City, couldn't be bothered waiting for the 8.20 and that was that.

RUCKER: What, you never went back?

BRASS: What for?

RUCKER: What about your Mum and all that.

BRASS: She kicked me out when she got married again. That was eight years ago. I was only sixteen. I've not seen or spoke to her since. I won't speak to her again either, the bitch.

RUCKER: Suppose she thought you'd wind the geezer up, eh?

BRASS: She caught the fat bastard raping me.

It was a Saturday morning. I'd just finished me paper round and went up to me room to get changed. Me an' me mates were going to Filbert Street — City was playing Arsenal — We always went when they played a cockney team. (*She smiles.*) I was just pouring the glue into a bag and the dirty fucker kicked me door in. He had the iron in one hand and a dirty book in the other.

RUCKER: Fucking hell.

BRASS: Made me suck him off while he looked at the readers' wives. That's when she came in. She got me with the iron — look. (*She lifts up her blouse at the back.*)

RUCKER: Fucking hell.

BRASS: After that I stayed with mates and all that for about a year — moved in with Claude. Next thing I know I'm on the game. Then I had the kid. That's when the pasting really started.

RUCKER: Didn't he want any kids?

BRASS: Not any white ones.

RUCKER: Bring the kid with you?

BRASS: Yeah. He's in a nursery. — He's starting school next year.

RUCKER: Got to be careful where you send 'im.

BRASS: Oh, I know. This nursery is lovely. Costs me fifty quid a week. Look I've got to go. I've just seen one — (*She looks off stage right.*)

RUCKER: Take care luv.

BRASS: What's your name?

RUCKER: Rucker, what's yours?

BRASS: Brass.

RUCKER: All right. See yer later Brass.

BRASS: Cheers, Rucker duck.

RUCKER *stands alone on the stage for a minute or so watching people walk past. He sees someone he knows on the top deck of a bus.*

RUCKER (*waving and smiling*): Cunt! (*He lights an Embassy.*)

SNEAKY (*as he enters from stage left*): He's not a bad feller that Polar.

RUCKER: Shame he's a scouse.

SNEAKY: Switch off Rucker. Serve anybody?

RUCKER: Nigerian, bangle. (*He hands* SNEAKY *a fiver, keeping a pound.*) Couple of Pakis came up messing the gear about.

SNEAKY: Should have told 'em to fuck off Rucker, don't stop weeding those Asians. Let's crack away, eh? It's bang on down there. (*He starts sorting out the gear in the case.*) Give your eyes a treat then Rucker. (RUCKER *moves up stage.* SNEAKY *pushes crates out and goes to work, now sitting on milk crate behind the case.*)

Here 'are now, stop. Here 'are now. look. (*He claps his hands.*) Stand your ground for thirty seconds. I'll show you what I am going to do. — Watch. You see this here. (*He holds up a watch.*) To go an buy off any high street jewellers — Ratners, Bravingtons — this would cost in the region of twenty-seven pounds. They're 9 carat rolled gold-plated. It's shock-proof, water proof, here — come in a bit closer luv. It's all right, I've had me breakfast, I won't bite you. That's it, put your right foot forward. Your left'll follow.

I've got a year's written guarantee, twenty-seven pounds' worth of commercial value absolutely free. F-R-double E, free of all cost and charge. We'll call it 'number one'. Number two, Selfridges sell 'em. They put 'un in fancy boxes and charge you fancy prices. I've got no fancy boxes — I've got no fancy prices. They're advertised on TV — believe they call the programme 'Police Five'.

Here it is. (*He holds aloft a pen.*) The Parker Papermate — genuine Parker pen, guaranteed to write ten thousand words. If it only does nine thousand, nine hundred and ninety-eight, come back and I'll tell you what the other two are. Parker pens are a world-wide concession and we got ours the same way as Selfridges and Harrods get theirs except they get theirs through the front door midday; we get ours through the back door midnight.

It comes in red, silver, black and blue and refills are sold throughout the world. If you want serving do it quickly and sharply 'cos if a policeman comes one way, me and the business go the other.

Bangle watches by Vogue, Parker Papermate pen. Thirty-nine pounds shop and store prices. Forget about thirty-nine. Forget about twenty-nine. The last and final sale of the day. Give me ten pounds to clear 'em out of the way!

Gentleman at the back there. Hold on there madam. Rick very lively. (*On 'rick', RUCKER moves forward and tries to buy. As he does so, he begins to concentrate on getting served rather than looking out. Suddenly he looks to the side of the stage and freezes.*)

RUCKER: Have it up.

SNEAKY: Where?

RUCKER: For your life.

With this, SNEAKY *moves from stage left with great urgency, pushing away imaginary customers and kicking crates back into the doorway.* SNEAKY *and* RUCKER *stand side by side in front of the crates and the now closed case. At this point a policeman enters stage left. He is uniformed, young and black, and he holds his helmet in his hands. He is creeping. When he sees he has been spotted by* SNEAKY *and* RUCKER *he puts his helmet back on and makes his way towards the centre of stage. He stops to talk to someone, he points indicating right turns, etc. Once free, feeling he is now too late to have any realistic chance of an arrest, he walks straight past them.*

SNEAKY: Don't fall asleep on the outside Rucker.

RUCKER: I wasn't falling asleep. I was trying to give you a rick.

SNEAKY: Try and keep your eyes open then, eh?

RUCKER: Well get yourself a proper rick then. What about that then, eh? A black cosser. Looked a right Rassie cunt and all.

SNEAKY: Well, he's got to be a right dog, ain't he. I mean, if you were black, would you be one?

RUCKER: No.

SNEAKY: There you are, then. You don't stand a chance with the white ones, so what chance you got with a schwarze?

RUCKER: None.

SNEAKY: Fuck him. Let's get to work.

(*As they get to work.*)

RUCKER: Have it up. It's Shaft.

(They move back to the doorway.)
PC YOUNG *enters from stage right.*
PC YOUNG: You might as well go now.
SNEAKY *(to RUCKER):* Oh, he's a monster, this cunt. *(To* PC YOUNG.*)* All right sarge. No value here.
PC YOUNG: Not with me here, it's not.
SNEAKY *(to RUCKER):* What a petty-minded fuck-dog eh? *(To* PC YOUNG.*)* Jumped off any buses lately?
PC YOUNG: I'm on till four, so I'll see you later. *(He exits.)*
SNEAKY: He's going to do my brain right in, that prick. *(Pause.)* There's something about him.
RUCKER: He's a cosser.
SNEAKY: No. It's more than that.
RUCKER: He's black.
SNEAKY: More.
RUCKER: He's a black cosser. He's a black cosser and he wants to nick you.
SNEAKY: That's it. That si wants to nick me. Is that a fuckin' liberty or what? *(Pause.)* Land fit for heroes. *(Pause.)* They were only supposed to work on the buses.
RUCKER: How could you be a black cosser?
SNEAKY: He's got to be the worse one I ever come across, straight.
RUCKER: What? Cosser or Luke?
SNEAKY: Both. The worse cossers before him were women. One nicked Vinnie Sharp's old man on the barrow.
RUCKER: He's about eighty.
SNEAKY: Yeah, he went under a wrong 'un. She's only searched him down the nick — found his pension

book on him. — They've stopped his pension — wanted by the DHSS and he's awaiting trial by jury for spitting in her face.
RUCKER: Somebody ought to help him out.
SNEAKY: We'll have a whip for him when he gets out.
RUCKER: Should try and stop him going in there.
SNEAKY: There's no value having a whip round before he goes in, 'cos then he won't have one when he comes out.
RUCKER: True.
SNEAKY: Pick the case up. Order what you want. I'm going down there. If it's bang on here, what's it gonna be like round Selfridges? If that fat Stevie ain't there, we'll work his plot. Meet me back here.
Exit first SNEAKY, *stage left, then* RUCKER *stage right with the case.* BRASS *enters from stage right. She stands around and after a minute* PC YOUNG *enters. He stands next to* BRASS.
PC YOUNG: Would you like some directions, miss?
BRASS: No thanks officer. You wouldn't happen to have a light though?
PC YOUNG: I do, as it happens. *(He pulls out a gold lighter.)*
BRASS: Dupoint?
PC YOUNG: Didn't I see you in court the other day?
BRASS: Court?
PC YOUNG: Yes, Marlborough Street.
BRASS: Probably. It's my work you see.
PC YOUNG: Just as I thought . . .
BRASS: Yes, I'm a store detective.
PC YOUNG: Oh. I thought you

were . . . you don't look like a store detective. More like a . . .

BRASS: Yes. I know. It's a disguise.

PC YOUNG: It's a good one. I'd give you thirty quid.

BRASS: Come on then. (*They laugh*.)

PC YOUNG: You'd probably get yourself more money.

BRASS: Ooh it makes my skin crawl.

PC YOUNG: What's the money like for a store detective?

BRASS: The money's fine, just not enough of it.

PC YOUNG: Same here. I want to make a career out of this job. Plenty of avenues open to an alert young man. They reckon I could be on the Regional Crime Squad in two years if I play my cards right.

BRASS: That's very important.

PC YOUNG: What?

BRASS: Playing your cards right.

PC YOUNG: My dad told me that years ago.

BRASS: Was he a policeman?

PC YOUNG: In Trinidad.

BRASS: Over here?

PC YOUNG: Schoolkeeper.

(*An imaginary customer walks past BRASS and leers at her.*)

Who's he?

BRASS: Nicked him last week.

PC YOUNG: Why was he leering at you like that?

BRASS: You know Catholics? (*He nods.*)

PC YOUNG: What for?

BRASS: Sunglasses.

PC YOUNG: See. Tell someone else, they'll tell you 'He's far too old to be stealing sunglasses'. Tell a policeman and he'll believe you,

'cos he'll know – professionalism.

BRASS: Reckoned he put them on 'cos his daughter wanted to see them on him. She started crying soon as he did, so he picked her up, gave her a pat here and there, generally consoling her, forgot about the sunglasses.

PC YOUNG (*laughing*): He expected you to stand for that. (*He laughs.*) He's guilty. You know what I think?

BRASS: What?

PC YOUNG: They're all guilty.

BRASS: Yeah, know what you mean.

PC YOUNG: It's true. They're all criminals. (*They look into the audience.*)

Pause.

Where did you catch him?

BRASS: Debenhams.

PC YOUNG: You're a long way from home.

BRASS: What?

PC YOUNG: Up here, Marble Arch.

BRASS: I'm on C & A today.

PC YOUNG: I thought you worked for Debenhams.

BRASS: I did last week.

PC YOUNG: That was quick.

BRASS: Yes. I'm with an agency.

PC YOUNG: That's good. What's it called?

BRASS: Effective Detective.

PC YOUNG: Fancy a drink soon?

BRASS: I don't think my fiancé would like that.

PC YOUNG: Oh yes. What does he do?

BRASS: Prison officer.

PC YOUNG: Plenty of overtime.

BRASS: We want our own place.

PC YOUNG: At his parents.

BRASS: No, mine. It drives him mad.

PC YOUNG: Independent, eh?

BRASS: Well, we've been there two years. Move into the house in five months. I'll be glad though. Nice to have a place of your own. Bit of security you know.

PC YOUNG: What boob?

BRASS: Scrubs.

PC YOUNG: They say you can earn yourself a few quid if you're a bright boy in the Scrubs.

BRASS: Well. He's not slow. Let's put it that way.

PC YOUNG: Any kids?

BRASS: No, not till we're older.

PC YOUNG: Best way, bit of security.

BRASS: He plays rugby.

PC YOUNG: So do I.

BRASS: Bit slim for rugby.

PC YOUNG: Eh? No way. I'm in the team.

BRASS: I got to shoot off.

PC YOUNG: Yeah. So have I.

They both exit in different directions. The stage is empty for a few seconds, then a young man – CAT – walks on wearing a dark blue tennis shirt, pink cotton crew-neck jumper, light blue cotton trousers, pleated at the top and pegged at the bottom, pink espadrilles; in his hand a small Floris bag. He is suntanned. He walks across stage checking it out, then walks off again.

Enter SNEAKY eating a MacDonalds'. He finishes it quickly, throwing the empty carton to the back of a shop doorway.

SNEAKY: Where is that si? Bollocks these 'Big Macs'. Got to have a quarter pounder. (*He exits carrying a cheeseburger, small fries and a coke.*)

Enter RUCKER. He stands in a shop doorway reading an Italian fashion magazine. He has the case with him and a bag containing coffees etc. Still reading, he lights an Embassy. Half a minute later, enter CAT. He stands unnoticed next to RUCKER for another half a minute or so.

CAT: He been nicked?

RUCKER (*looking up*): Oh. All right Cat?

CAT: Sweet.

RUCKER: No. He's gone up Selfridges.

CAT: What's that then? (*He indicates the magazine.*)

RUCKER: Nothing (*Hiding it.*)

CAT: Don't drive me mad. It's this quarters.

RUCKER *hands it over.*

Where did you get this?

RUCKER: Down there.

CAT: A bottle.

RUCKER: Carpet.

CAT: For the sake of a carpet I might as well steal it myself. For another cows, I could buy one.

RUCKER: They're a ching.

CAT: Straight? (*He looks at the price tag.*) What a liberty, eh? A fucking ching. (*He hands over three pounds.*) You're still batty Rucker.

RUCKER (*Counting the money*): Yeah. All right. It's all bollocks that, anyway.

CAT: Yeah. Why's that?

RUCKER: It's all in Italian.

CAT: That's all right. I speak Raddie.

RUCKER: Yeah, all right.

CAT: Yeah. All right. Chinned anyone lately?

RUCKER: Paki, this morning.

CAT: Don't really count, though, does it?

RUCKER: Yeah. Put just as much effort in with a Paki. Just as much concentration. You could stop counting drunk Paddies, irons. They all count, Cat.

CAT: You should get some readies out of it.

RUCKER: Got an apple for just chinning somebody last night.

CAT: Who did you chin?

RUCKER: Some bubble with a Merc. Kept parking it outside me uncle's gaff.

CAT: Shrewd move. (*He watches someone walk across the stage.*) I'll see you later. (*He leaves the magazine.*)

RUCKER *sits down on the milk crates, starts looking at the magazine and eating a roll. There follows a pause of about a minute. There is a commotion to his left.*

RUCKER: Oi. Leave her alone. Yes, you fats. (*Standing.*) You're all right − digging birds out. Come on ya mug. I'll tear your fuckin' nose off.

(*He walks towards where the action is.*)

You all right Brass?

BRASS: Yeah, ta Rucker. A-rab bastard. He wanted it for fifteen quid. Mind you, I could do with fifteen quid. I don't want to miss those carpet men.

RUCKER: You want some cheese and tomato roll?

BRASS: No, ta duck.

RUCKER: Tea? (*Offering her a paper mug.*)

BRASS: Sugar?

RUCKER: Three.

BRASS: Hot and sweet. Lovely. (*She takes the cup.*) Ooh nice.

RUCKER: Wanna fag?

BRASS (*takes one*): Smashing.

RUCKER: I ain't got a light though.

BRASS: I got one here somewhere. (*She begins rummaging through her bag.*) Can't find 'em. Sodding Durex.

RUCKER (*looking into her bag*): Fuck me. How much does that lot come to?

BRASS: Fuck all really. I get 'em wholesale over Shoreditch.

RUCKER: There's a lighter.

BRASS: Oh yeah, that black cosser gave me a tug.

RUCKER: What's he say?

BRASS: I told him I was a store detective. (*She watches something pass.*) Do you like that Rucker?

RUCKER: Cadillac?

BRASS: Yeah.

RUCKER: No, they're shit. I'd get a BMW 7.01 − good motor.

BRASS: Can you drive?

RUCKER: Yeah. Took me mate's test for him.

BRASS: I can't.

RUCKER: I'll teach you.

BRASS: How?

RUCKER: We'll use me mate's car, sweet.

BRASS: You sound like him, moany bollocks.

RUCKER: It just slips out when you're up here all day, just takes over. Sneaky never turns off. He must have forgotten what it was like being a fuckin' human − like caterpillars, except they turn into spivs.

BRASS: What are you going to do then, Rucker?

RUCKER: Banks.

BRASS: No, really.

RUCKER: Well, let's say building societies. They're for wankers really. Someone invented them for people that can't rob banks. I could rob banks but I'm better off robbing, say, a few building societies. Get a fair run before I'm nicked. After about ten, say four thousand per go, that's forty thousand pounds. By this time, I'll be seventeen. I am sixteen and a bit – a half – now. I'll get about seven years. I'll do two in Borstal, another two in the nick and I'm out. Still only twenty-one.

BRASS: Ten thousand a year.

RUCKER: More than that, 'cos the money'll be earning interest. Plus I can do a City and Guilds apprenticeship in there – bricklaying, something like that.

BRASS: That's true. That's a good plan, Rucker.

RUCKER: And if I don't fancy doing four years, I could just turn supergrass and do plastering instead.

BRASS: Every fucker's a supergrass these days.

RUCKER: I'll bet there'll be police supergrasses soon.

BRASS: *Sunday Mirror*, American Bank, Brixton riots, the black kid in Stoke Newington – down to us. Yes, McNee is a member of the KKK.

RUCKER: Political ones. The sole purpose of the Falklands was the mug vote. Yes, we are going to abolish the National Health Service.

BRASS: Cruise missiles are here to stay. Ronald Reagan told me so.

I've seen one Rucker. Got to go. (*She goes.*)

RUCKER *looks at the magazine.*
SNEAKY *walks on from stage right, eating a MacDonalds'.*

SNEAKY: Let's crack away.
(RUCKER *moves to look-out position,* SNEAKY *pulls out crates, etc. and claps his hands.*)

We're gonna sort out the spyers from the buyers, the shoppers from the shop-lifters. Wholesale, retail, bloody well blackmail. We're gonna sort out the spyers from the buyers. Shoppers from shop-lifters. We'll call this Number One – bangle watch by Bolex. It's nine carat, rolled, gold-plated. With a year's guarantee, not by me but by the manufacturer. It's the same watch that's sold by Ratners and Bravingtons, only difference being they put it in a fancy box and charge you the earth for it. Well, you can't wear the box on your arm. It comes with an indestructible interlocking clasp. Get one for your girlfriend. If she's already got one you can sell it to the wife. Twenty-seven shop and store price, that's Number One.

Here's Number Two – the De Luxe Executive Papermate by Parker. I don't need to tell you too much about this. As you can see, it's a genuine Parker pen, renowned throughout the western world. Selfridges stock 'em. They'll charge you twelve pounds for it. Comes complete with refill. If you want serving, do it quickly before that policeman comes, 'cos if I get six months for selling, I'm sure you don't want three for buying. To the first dozen buyers. When these are gone, there'll be no more, and if you're Number Thirteen, you'll feel like the man that fell out of the balloon. You just won't be in it.

They've got to be cleared the quick way – the quick way being the jolly cheap way. Thirty-nine pounds' worth of commercial value – I'll take ten pounds.

For the next ten minutes or so SNEAKY *is busy taking money.* RUCKER *looks out anxiously.*

RUCKER: Live-o. Co' the other side. (*They clear everything away*.)

SNEAKY: That was a good edge, that.

RUCKER: It's bang on.

CAT *enters stage left.*

SNEAKY: Cat?

CAT: Listen Rucker. Do us a favour mate. Get a cold Perrier from that gaff round the corner. What you want Sneak?

SNEAKY: Same. No get me a cold Swan.

CAT: Cold Perrier, cold Swan and whatever you want for yourself. (RUCKER *starts to leave*.) Oh, yeah and a large packet of Rizlas and a straw from MacDonalds. Cheers Rucker.

SNEAKY: Got some charlie, Cat?

CAT: Here are. Standing here fanning to Rucker, I seen this Richard. Now she's a right regular up the Zanzibar. Tried to cop for it once and she blanked me. Anyway she's gone past. I thought I'd try and cop for it again. I'm on her hay, and she's a floater. Well, she's got to have something ain't she? (SNEAKY *nods*.) Look. (CAT *shows* SNEAKY *the inside of an envelope*.)

SNEAKY: Fuck me. Is that all charlie?

CAT: Yes. There's an ounce. I weighed it on those electric scales in a Paki shop. It's about four grams as it happens. That's not all though. Have a look at these. (*He hands* SNEAKY *some notes*.)

SNEAKY: Three hundred quid.

You've had a result, Cat.

CAT: I've got another fourteen here.

SNEAKY: What you trying to do to me? So you've had a touch. You've sent my outside man away, stopped me working, just to do my brain in?

CAT: Slow down Sneaky. I am trying to put you in it.

SNEAKY: Nice fella – gets two grand, gives his pal a line of charlie.

CAT: No . . . look at the numbers. (SNEAKY *does so*.)

SNEAKY: They're all the same.

(*At this point,* PC YOUNG *is creeping up on them*.)

CAT: You're a live wire, straight. I'll give you fifteen pounds for everyone you change up.

SNEAKY: Sweet.

PC YOUNG: You're nicked.

Scene Two

CAT: Quoi?

PC YOUNG: Arrested.

CAT: Moi?

PC YOUNG: No, him.

SNEAKY: What for?

PC YOUNG: Street trading without a licence and obstructing the highway.

SNEAKY: I was giving him directions.

PC YOUNG: If you don't come now I'll call the van.

SNEAKY: Can't even give a fella a few directions without getting nicked. He weren't too far out that George Oral.

PC YOUNG: Orwell.

SNEAKY: Come straight into it, didn't cha, typical cosser.

PC YOUNG (*going for his radio*): Yeah. All right.

SNEAKY: Leave it out Sarge.

PC YOUNG: I saw you take his money. You're nicked. (SNEAKY *and* CAT *look at one another.* CAT *indicates he should take the nick.*)

SNEAKY: All right Sarge.

PC YOUNG: What?

SNEAKY: It's only cricket, you saw me take his money.

(PC YOUNG *stops using his radio.*)

PC YOUNG: Righto — come on then.

They start to exit stage left. CAT *stage right. As each party is about to leave the stage* PC YOUNG *calls out to* CAT.

PC YOUNG: Excuse me, Mussirr, mussirr!

CAT: Pardong?

PC YOUNG *signals him to come over.* CAT *does so.*

PC YOUNG (*to* SNEAKY): You're unbelievable.

SNEAKY: What?

PC YOUNG (*to* CAT): This one like rat, wee?

CAT: My English little but this rat he look like.

PC YOUNG: Now give this man his money back. (SNEAKY *hands* CAT *a ten pound note. As he does,* PC YOUNG's *radio comes into action telling him to move very quickly into Park Lane where a jeweller's is being robbed. He exits.*)

SNEAKY: It's a film.

CAT: You wouldn't think so.

SNEAKY: What a fanny, eh?

CAT: He's alert him.

SNEAKY: He's double alert. (*They laugh.*) Though he was right on us there, straight.

Enter RUCKER *stage left.*

CAT: Here's Rucker.

RUCKER (*to* CAT): Here are. (*To* SNEAKY.) Here are.

CAT: What about the straw?

RUCKER: Nearest MacDonald's is there. (*He points to the right.*)

SNEAKY: Hang on Rucker. While you're up there, cash this in for five cockles.

RUCKER: Where?

SNEAKY (*handing him a note*): Bureau de Change.

RUCKER: Yeah, all right. (*He exits.*)

CAT: Too strong, Sneak.

SNEAKY: No. He's still a juvenile — won't get bird. Anyway it's the best move all round. If he takes it, it's got to be good. He's one suspicious Paki up there.

CAT: If he's not back in eight minutes, it's every man for himself.

SNEAKY: Hang on taxi — oi, hang on.

CAT: Fuck me, Sneaky, no need for panic.

(SNEAKY *runs over to the taxi, off stage, and comes back on smiling. He hands* CAT *thirty-five pounds.*)

You know they're all grasses, them slags.

SNEAKY: My part. Wait here. Give us the others (CAT *hands him the money.*)

CAT: Wait here and take the counterfeiting nick, shall I?

SNEAKY: Have you got any counterfeit money on you?

CAT: No.

SNEAKY: So what difference?

CAT: Just an ounce of cocaine.

SNEAKY: Well, they're not interested in that, are they?

CAT: Live-o then, Sneak.

SNEAKY: See you later. (*He exits.*)

(CAT *uses the time to roll a joint. After a pause* RUCKER *gets back.*)

CAT: Sweet?

RUCKER: Yeah. Here are. (*He hands him a straw.*)

CAT: Oh, yeah, nice.

RUCKER: Where's he gone?

CAT: Dunno. You want a line of charlie, Rucker?

RUCKER: No.

CAT: Why's that?

RUCKER: Don't take drugs. Strictly for mugs.

CAT: Can't make you wrong, Rucker. Got to be buzzing though. (CAT *is somehow organising himself a line of charlie. He makes a line: it is pure cocaine; something to which* CAT *is totally unaccustomed. He is silent.* RUCKER *looks on.*)

CAT (*toasting*): Me say you an you – ya love de badness. For true dem ave ter run, when radication come. Cocaine may blow your brain.

RUCKER: But being Rucker is. Frey live in a Marble Arch.

CAT: This gear is fucking mental. Cruise missile powder. Can you roll a joint?

RUCKER: Yeah.

CAT: I give you a bottle to roll a joint.

RUCKER: All right.

(CAT *hands him two pounds and joint paraphernalia.*)

CAT: If you could vote, who would you vote for?

RUCKER: They're all liars.

CAT: Born Communist.

RUCKER: You reckon?

CAT: You got to be. 'They're all liars' – right left-wing whine to it.

RUCKER: You're right. I am a bit red as it happens. I fucking hate Margaret Thatcher. I'd vote for Yosser.

CAT: He's a right mug, the cunt. Everyone's lapping him up. He's a right egg. Bilko's a different matter.

RUCKER: All right Cat.

CAT: You ever go ticket gaffs?

RUCKER: Yeah.

CAT: Get anything?

RUCKER: What he gives me.

CAT: Jekyll paymaster, ain't he?

RUCKER: Better than John on the corner.

CAT (*laughing*): What's he like, John?

RUCKER: A right dog. (*More laughter.*)

CAT: Won't pull up a dollar, the cunt. Won't go out the Bricklayers Arms. On Tillie's birthday everybody's got a bottle of gear bar him. He's a dog. (*More giggles.*) Who else you worked for? (*He lights the joint.*)

RUCKER (*beginning to join in*): The Brain and Baby Brain.

(CAT *just laughs.*)

RUCKER: They're too busy buying everything up.

CAT (*imitating The Brain*): 'All right, Goldie, we'll have it all'. (RUCKER *laughs.*) 'Seen 'im smelly Ray?'

Bit of a red eh? You want to watch that. You'll end up skint.

RUCKER: Plenty of lefties with readies.

CAT: And they hold right on to it. They're all like that Vanessa Redgrave sending their kids to public school. They're the worse kind of frauds you can get. People are socialist for two reasons – guilt or just plain ignorance. All these

people do is complain. It ain't hard
to go and get a few quid. If a
factory closes down, they're fucked.
They got no initiative, the
Northerners or Vanessa Redgrave.
The best thing we could do is bomb
simultaneously — Russia, China,
Libya, eradicate the enemy, simple.

RUCKER: They'd bomb us back.

CAT: No they wouldn't. They'd be
dead.

RUCKER: They've got early-warning
radar and all that.

CAT: Wee, we'd still be sweet, 'cos if
they had time to bomb anybody,
they'd do the Yanks, by the time
they got round to us, they'd be
dust.

RUCKER: That's true.

CAT: It'll take them years to think of
that.

You ever go football?

RUCKER: It's for mugs.

CAT: Yeah, yeah, forty years old
gangster. It's for mugs. It's a right
laugh.

RUCKER: You go?

CAT: Tickets. You'd love it.
Everybody kicking each other's
heads in. Cutting cossers.
Right up your street.

RUCKER: I couldn't have a fight over
a football match. It's stupid. I went
once over QPR against Luton.
Nobody wears any scarves. We just
chinning everybody.

CAT: Who's we, Rucker?

RUCKER: Egbo.

CAT: Who's that, Edgware Road?

RUCKER: You got it.

CAT: All schwarzers or what?

RUCKER: Lot of blacks — lot of
whites.

CAT: Who der ruck with?

RUCKER: Anybody.

CAT: Archway?

RUCKER: We had it off with them at
the Lyceum.

CAT: Straight.

RUCKER: Yeah. They're all Arsenal.

CAT: Naughty.

RUCKER: They thought they were.

CAT: You do 'em?

RUCKER: I think so; none of our lot
got done.

CAT: What about the Angel?

RUCKER: They're all right.

CAT: Have a line of charlie.

RUCKER: No thanks.

CAT: I'm having one. Do you drink
Rucker?

RUCKER: Drinking stops you
thinking.

CAT: Where do you get all these
from?

RUCKER: I sussed it. It's not hard to
work out is it? My mate's brother
sells that shit. Don't know what
day of the week it is half the time.
I found him asleep last week curled
up on the carpet, straw sticking out
of his nose, joint in his mouth with
a fried egg and some chips stuck on
his back. Cocaine. It's all bollocks.

CAT (*makes his line*): I could make
another ounce out of this and some
baby powder. Still be the best gear
around. It's strong. Be the
Edmundo of the coke world.

Cocaine may blow your brain
But being Rucker is irie.

RUCKER: Look pon me berrie
Seen it was green

CAT: Say red boy where is the M16?

(*Enter* BRASS. *As she does,* CAT
starts toasting.)

Oh gal, the way you walk-a-do
Because the whole world turn
    against you,
Tell her say me sorry, tell her me
    missing her madly
Tell her me life getting lonely . . .

BRASS: Rucker. Cat.

CAT (*with a black American accent*):
Say, what's happening?

BRASS: A lot down Park Lane. I just
see a jewellery shop get done. I had
one an' all – a Nigerian, one foot
in the taxi and suddenly there's
coppers everywhere. He shit
himself, the African.

CAT: Probably the chief's son.

RUCKER: Probably the chief's dad.

BRASS: I think he was the chief. Gave
me twenty pounds to leave him
alone when he saw photographers
appearing from the sewers.

CAT: I know and you know that this
love is really really true. Don't
change your style, stop your
running wild, 'cos you're just a
runaway child.

BRASS: You got to remember – that
you're just another Cat, so baby
look at that.

CAT (*rolling a joint*): Fancy a line of
charlie?

BRASS (*heavy sarcasm*): I'll have four.

CAT: Sweet. Rucker would you go
and get us a bottle of gear – Moet
– make sure it's cold.

RUCKER: You taking the piss?

CAT: I'll sort you something out –
and some paper cups.

RUCKER: How many?

CAT: Well, you'll want a glass of
champagne, won't you?

(RUCKER *looks at* BRASS *then
nods*.)

Here are. (CAT *gives him a twenty
pound note. Exit* RUCKER.)

Did you see any black policemen
down there?

BRASS: He was one of the first on the
scene.

CAT: You know the one I mean?

BRASS: Yes, he's always up here.

CAT: Right si.

BRASS: That's him. Thinks I'm a
store detective.

CAT: Thinks I'm a Frenchman.
There's your charlie.

BRASS (*moves round to the cocaine*):
There's four lines there.

CAT: That's what you wanted.

BRASS: I can't do all that lot. I'll
be giving it away.

CAT: Do you do that?

BRASS: Not often. (CAT *laughs. She
does two lines.*) Fucking Ada. What
is that stuff?

CAT: Blinding gear, eh?

BRASS: Where's Rucker got to with
that champagne? Hang on, there's
rat brain. (CAT *looks up to see*
SNEAKY *entering stage left.* CAT
is laughing his head off.)

SNEAKY: Sweet. Done the lot. Cost
me an apple. They've all been
nicked on Selfridges. Denus's got
two, ricks, right. An' the General's
got two. (CAT *nods, still laughing.*)
Gave 'em a ching apiece – five
magaratts each. Sent 'em into
Selfridges, Debenhams, Marks 'n'
Sparks and the one with four into
D H Evans. So that's your neves.
(*He hands* CAT £700.) And this is
mine (£260.)

CAT: Line of charlie there, if you
want it.

SNEAKY: Yeah. All right. Where's
Rucker?

CAT: Gone for some champers, old
man.

SNEAKY: I've got to work here for fuck's sake.

CAT: You just got a carpet.

SNEAKY: There's four hours left. I can get rid of this shit. Where's that line?

CAT: There's two there. (*He points.*)

SNEAKY (*snorts a line of cocaine*): Let's go horseriding.

CAT: Let's do this bottle of gear.

SNEAKY: We going to loz the Richard?

BRASS: We'd rather loz you.

SNEAKY: Don't drive me mad luv.

BRASS: Don't 'luv' me, you creep.

SNEAKY: I'll knock her out in a minute.

CAT (*laughing*): Let's have a drink.

SNEAKY: I hate warm champagne.

CAT: He's going to get it chilled.

SNEAKY: What about glasses?

CAT: She's going to get some out of there. (*He hands BRASS a fiver. She exits.*)

SNEAKY: You're not going to rump that, are you?

CAT: 'Course I'm not going to rump it. She probably wouldn't have it anyway.

SNEAKY: I give her forty quid.

CAT: I tell you what, you're one horrible person, Sneaky.

SNEAKY: My part. (*Pause.*) I don't make myself out a nice fellow.

CAT: What, are you sensitive?

SNEAKY: Sensitive to a pound note.

CAT: I heard you got nicked breaking into a ching in the city club last week.

SNEAKY: You don't get any medals for spending money Cat.

CAT: It's good for the economy.

SNEAKY: Here. Look, the sex goddess.

BRASS (*entering*): They've got some really nice ones in there. I got these, cut plastic.

SNEAKY: I'm not drinking out of a plastic cup.

BRASS: Sod you then.

CAT: I should go up to Mothercare and get a bottle with a tit on it. You can drink out of that.

SNEAKY: You got a light, luv?

BRASS: Yeah.

SNEAKY: Sweet. (BRASS *throws her eyes up.*)

Enter RUCKER.

CAT: The man. The man of the hour. Ladies and gentlemen, the man you've all been waiting for . . . Did you fuck her, Rucker?

RUCKER: Had to go down to Bond Street. Got this. (*He has an ice bucket with two bottles of champagne.*) I've been to about six different gaffs putting salt on it.

SNEAKY: Best buck up the whole street, him.

CAT: West Lon-don.

BRASS: My hero. (*She kisses him.*)

RUCKER: Nice one, Brass.

SNEAKY: Never mind the love story. Open the gear. Look at this Gills. He can't believe it. (*They all look up and jeer at somebody on the bus.*)

CAT: The old straight-goer, eh?

RUCKER: Busy.

SNEAKY: Easily content.

BRASS: I've never met one.

SNEAKY: That charlie knocked the top of my head. Fill it up.

(*He moves to* BRASS.)

BRASS: Fuck the carpet men.

RUCKER: Get a reduction. (*General laughter.*)

SNEAKY: If it's the same firm that did mine, they'll charge you. (*More laughs.*)

CAT: That's a funny old game, brassing.

BRASS: Pick pocketing must be a funny old sort of game too, really.

CAT: It has its moments. In fact, I'd say it's the best job I've ever had. Lot of irregular hours involved. I don't mind though, I'm happy.

SNEAKY: But you can't reign forever, Cat.

CAT: I'll retire when I'm thirty. Don't want to be fucked about working when you're that age.

RUCKER: You'll get bored.

CAT: I'll have kids.

BRASS: I've got a kid. They're murder.

CAT: Few people have said that.

BRASS: This is not a good place to bring a kid up in. Not any more.

SNEAKY: It's never been any good if you're skint. You're up for none as soon as they spank your arse.

RUCKER: He's dead fucking right you know.

BRASS: I know.

CAT: Still, it's better than Russia.

RUCKER: That's what the papers say and they only print what they want you to read.

SNEAKY: Bar none.

RUCKER: I might go into politics.

CAT: Secretary of State for rucking.

BRASS (*taking plastic glass*): There's that copper. I've got to move. He thinks I'm a store detective. (*She exits.*)

Enter PC YOUNG *from the other side. He is not creeping with his helmet off but walking leisurely.*

PC YOUNG: Party chaps?

CAT: You would like, eh?

PC YOUNG: No thank you, sir. I'm on duty. (*To* SNEAKY.) What's going on?

SNEAKY: He just got out of a cab five minutes ago – give us a glass each and opened the bottle. He's got to be a right pot-house. Catch any jewel thieves?

PC YOUNG: No, the bastards got away.

RUCKER: What about the car number plates?

PC YOUNG: Is he old enough to be drinking that stuff?

SNEAKY: Yeah, yeah. He's thirty-two next month.

PC YOUNG: What was that rattie? An attempt at humour?

CAT: In Paris, me toe. (*He points to* PC YOUNG's *uniform.*)

PC YOUNG: You carry gun?

CAT: Quoi?

PC YOUNG (*making the shape of a gun with his hands*): Bang! Bang!

CAT: Ah, oui. Yes, gons.

PC YOUNG: Vital to police work. This country very stupid . . . me no gon.

SNEAKY: What do you want a gun for?

PC YOUNG: Well, for years they weren't needed, but you've got to face facts. Things have changed, and, under the new no foul system, the police should be armed.

SNEAKY: So, if you have a gun you can shoot me?

PC YOUNG: Well, it'd save taking you to court every day.

SNEAKY: A bad guy, eh?
Why didn't you join the army?

PC YOUNG: Why didn't you?

SNEAKY: I don't need to join any of that bollocks. I make my own money. People with your mentality join the army.

PC YOUNG: Your type are busy selling American cigarettes.

RUCKER: How can you be black and be an old bill?

PC YOUNG: What are you, black? Typical arsehole question.

SNEAKY: I don't know. He's not wrong, is he? If I was black I couldn't be a cosser.

PC YOUNG: You couldn't be one as you are. It's a good job . . . Why shouldn't I be a policeman?

SNEAKY: It's against the grain. What about when you fancy a joint, bit of the old sensie?

PC YOUNG: People want to smoke it, it's up to them. It doesn't bother me. I just nick 'em.

RUCKER: You got any Scottish blood?

PC YOUNG: Strictly Trinidadian.

SNEAKY: Don't you notice the other Rastas being a bit narrow-minded when it comes to black police?

PC YOUNG: What's to stop them joining?

RUCKER: 'Cos they're probably fitted up for sus at six years-old.

PC YOUNG: They've abolished that now.

(CAT *lays out a spoonful of charlie behind* PC YOUNG's *back*.)

RUCKER: And look what they've given us now — attempted theft from persons unknown.

PC YOUNG: That's the way it goes.

SNEAKY: No point talking to him, is there. He's just another ninety pounds-a-week mug.

PC YOUNG: That's all you know. Buffoon. (*He starts to walk off*.)

CAT: Auv-war musseewer.

PC YOUNG: Yeah. All right Frenchie. (*He exits*.)

RUCKER: He's an animal.

SNEAKY: What a robot.

CAT: Born cosser.

SNEAKY: You're not wrong.

CAT: What a downer. Imagine eight of them coming in your peter.

RUCKER: All you've got is a blanket.

SNEAKY: No sleep, forty-nine hours.

RUCKER: No food.

CAT: No salmon. Every three hours one of them comes into your cell and says stupid things.

SNEAKY: What's your mate's name?

RUCKER: Tell us in your own words then, son. How you stabbed the queer.

SNEAKY: Well, you're not getting bail.

RUCKER: Does your mum know you're a yobbo?

CAT: So, you were waiting at the bus stop in order to catch the bus. You expect us to swallow that?

SNEAKY: We know you're a thief. Your old man's a thief.

RUCKER: See yourself as a hard man do you?

CAT: Glad I've never been nicked.

SNEAKY: You got no cons?

CAT: Straight.

SNEAKY: What about those cashmeres with Billy Starr?

CAT: Never got to court.

SNEAKY: You were caught bang to rights.

CAT: We were only juveniles. Got a caution. Billy's old man's the Edmundo at the nick. Result really. All I want to do now is get the flat paid for. Sell it when we go to

Aussie.

SNEAKY: They're a bit strict.

CAT: They got a right to be. Don't want the wrong type over there. If they weren't strict about who they let in, we wouldn't be going there.

SNEAKY: Everybody's getting chucked out of there now, Cat. Be double boring. You'd have to fanny to the natives.

RUCKER (*with an Aussie accent*): All right Cat, ya fuckin' Pom. Have a Fosters.

SNEAKY: Start asking for champagne out there, they'll string you up.

RUCKER: Fucking poofter.

SNEAKY: This is bollocks. We ain't going to get to work here. Let's go horse-riding.

CAT: I dunno.

SNEAKY: Sauna?

CAT: Hooky?

SNEAKY: Hooky, if you want hooky.

CAT: Sauna. I dunno.

SNEAKY: Let's go drinking.

CAT: Let's go drinking.

SNEAKY: Where?

CAT: I dunno. Let's get a sandie. I want a jay. Hold on. Oi, Rucker, did they have a women's one of those in that gaff? (*Pointing to a magazine.*)

RUCKER: Yeah.

CAT: Go and get us one.

RUCKER: They're a ching.

CAT: Yeah. Here y'are. (*He hands him a fiver. Exit* RUCKER.)

SNEAKY: Live-o Rucker. What time is it?

CAT: Half-two.

SNEAKY: It's spark out here now.

CAT: Like the Gobi desert.

SNEAKY: Have a look – it's Linda Lovelace.

BRASS (*entering*): Gonna piss down any minute. What time is it?

SNEAKY: Time you had a watch.

BRASS: He might look like a horrible no-good ponced-up slag, but his humour's so good he gets away with it. I wouldn't bother asking you the time. Your clock stopped in 1969 when you were ten years-old. Knew God was on your side when we went decimal – quicker to count your money. Bet you sat next to the rich kid in the class, nicking all his stuff. Kicking all the girls. Went to his house, looked up his Mum's dress. You haven't changed, you're doing the same things. The only difference is, you're bitter about it now.

SNEAKY: Yeah, all right.

(CAT *laughs.*)

BRASS: I feel sorry for your missus.

SNEAKY: I don't think she'd envy you much.

CAT: It's raining.

SNEAKY: See, the wicked witch of the North.

BRASS: Cockney bastard.

CAT: Ooh, all together. (*Football chant.*)

SNEAKY: Where's that si gone?

BRASS: You talking about Rucker?

SNEAKY: No, Lord Lucan.

CAT: Yes, he's talking about Rucker.

BRASS: I know he wouldn't see quality if it spanked him straight in the gob, the cunt.

SNEAKY: See, this is down to you.

CAT: What is?

SNEAKY: She's worked here months and I never had to have any fucking contact. Sweet. From now on she'll be stopping to swap abuse every time she passes.

CAT: I'm bored with this.

SNEAKY: Let's smise.

CAT: No, wait for Rucker.

SNEAKY: Look at that rain.

CAT: I think this cocaine's completely taken over. Feel like jumping under one of those buses.

BRASS: You need something to eat, sit down.

CAT: I know, but every time I decide what to have, it makes me feel sick.

SNEAKY: You took too much of it.

CAT: How can you take too much charlie?

(BRASS *takes fags from her handbag.* CAT *buzzes her wallet.*)

BRASS: Give it back, Cat.

CAT: What?

BRASS: Come on, stop fucking about.

CAT: What?

BRASS: That's my carpet money.

Enter PC YOUNG.

PC YOUNG: What's all this?

BRASS: He's driving me mad.

SNEAKY: He's only having a laugh.

BRASS: Are you going to give it back?

CAT: What?

BRASS: Right, Rucker.

(RUCKER *re-enters carrying Italian Vogue.*)

RUCKER: What's happening?

BRASS: He nicked me purse. Me dad gave it to me.

RUCKER: Give it back or I'll knock you out.

SNEAKY: Oh, switch off, you ice.

(RUCKER *hits* SNEAKY *over the head with the magazine.* SNEAKY *in turn falls to the floor.* PC YOUNG *stands around looking, a bit lost.*)

PC YOUNG: Come on. Let's calm down a bit.

RUCKER (*to* CAT): You – give it back to her.

(*To* PC YOUNG.) You – can go and nick someone on brollies.

(*As* RUCKER *speaks to* PC YOUNG, CAT *chins* RUCKER. PC YOUNG *stands motionless.*)

BRASS: Well, do something you soppy bastard.

PC YOUNG *grabs* CAT *and tries to use a police arm lock.* CAT *in turn pulls out his knife and stabs the copper.* BRASS *and* RUCKER *run off.* RUCKER *is aided by* BRASS.

Taxi! Taxi!

SNEAKY *runs off in the opposite direction. He remembers his case.*

SNEAKY: Oh, me peter.

He turns and runs back, to find CAT *standing over* PC YOUNG, *pulling gold chains out of the policeman's helmet, which has fallen off his head.*

Put us in it, Cat.

Lights go down.

COMING APART

For my father

Characters

ANNE KATHERIN
IRMA
GEORGE
MR HANUSSEN

Scene One

On the stairway of the apartment house. IRMA, *laden with bags, is coming home from work.* ANNE KATHERIN *comes up behind her.*

ANNE KATHERIN: What's that noise?

IRMA: What?

ANNE KATHERIN: It can't be lorries can it? This isn't the right road.

IRMA: Excuse me.

ANNE KATHERIN: Must be from the construction site, noise travels in this weather. What do you think of the new blocks up there? They'll stick the Turks in of course.

ANNE KATHERIN *passes in front of* IRMA *and turns round.*

That's a lot of bags. Been shopping? Been on a binge?

IRMA: It's only food I'm afraid.

ANNE KATHERIN: You must eat enough, like a horse judging by — I used to myself but I don't now. You're thin though.

IRMA: Yes.

ANNE KATHERIN: My name's Anne Katherin. I've just moved in. Well last week but I only got the last of my furniture in today. Not seen you around so I couldn't introduce myself before.

IRMA: I'm pleased to meet you.

ANNE KATHERIN: And you're Irma Hoffener. It's okay, I got your name from the board downstairs. I've figured out who's who pretty much already. Names to faces. I don't know how long I'll be living here, it's hard to tell.

IRMA: It's a pleasant house.

ANNE KATHERIN: Have you been here long?

IRMA: Over twenty years.

IRMA *picks up her bags again, ready to carry on up the stairs.* ANNE KATHERIN *keeps talking.* IRMA *replaces her bags after a while.*

ANNE KATHERIN: I'm not from Berlin either though I've been here, God, five years. Where does the time go? I've a job starting in the autumn so maybe I'll be here forever. I hated it at home anyway. I'm well out of that. Even so, it's a strange city don't you think?

IRMA: You live in a place so long . . .

ANNE KATHERIN: Sometimes I think it's strange but then what do I know? I've been to Paris once and Holland for the summer two years ago. I think it's important to travel but somehow I don't.

IRMA: That's often the case.

ANNE KATHERIN: What?

IRMA: You must excuse me.

ANNE KATHERIN: Any of the people living here OK? I mean a lot of them are a bit 'past it' looking.

IRMA: It's usually very quiet.

ANNE KATHERIN: You can tell that just looking at the place. It's built the same as the others on the street but the whole feeling's different. I'm sensitive to atmospheres.

IRMA: Are you?

ANNE KATHERIN: In buildings I mean. I'm not so hot on people. I had an uncle who was an architect. I never met him, he was my mother's brother. I gave up wanting to be one myself years ago. It's crazy the number of things I've wanted to be. Some were fads but I was really serious about some of them. Like the time I wanted to be a mission doctor.

IRMA: You would have to train for a long time I imagine.

ANNE KATHERIN: Forever but that

wasn't the problem. I could have travelled as well, not to the usual places but Africa and that kind of thing. I had to forget the whole thing when I gave up that Christian crap.

IRMA: You could still have become a doctor.

ANNE KATHERIN: That was another very good reason for getting away from home. They were obsessive about it. I mean unhealthy.

IRMA: I'm sorry to hear that.

ANNE KATHERIN: Oh don't worry about it. They enjoy it no end. It's just me. I didn't. To be honest it just strikes me as silly — all that moaning and groaning.

IRMA: Very.

ANNE KATHERIN: You're not religious then?

IRMA: Religious?

ANNE KATHERIN: Good for you, it's unusual though for someone of your age.

IRMA: Is it?

ANNE KATHERIN: Of course it is. Well maybe less here than — elsewhere. It probably depends on where you come from as much as anything.

IRMA: Perhaps, yes.

ANNE KATHERIN: Well what else could it be?

IRMA: I don't know, I suppose I've not really given it much thought.

ANNE KATHERIN: It's important to keep thinking and questioning. It's easy for the mind to become atrophied.

IRMA: I'm usually very tired in the evenings.

ANNE KATHERIN: Just in from work I suppose?

IRMA: Yes that's right. I had to go and get the shopping done first of course.

ANNE KATHERIN: Do that every night do you? Work, shopping, home?

IRMA: Yes.

ANNE KATHERIN: So what do you work at, is it far?

IRMA: I usually walk there in the mornings but come the evening you get tired so I take a bus.

ANNE KATHERIN: That's the opposite of me. I'm worse than useless in the mornings, it's only about now that I liven up. You should see me round midnight. What do you think of the rent?

IRMA: I can afford it.

ANNE KATHERIN: I suppose they're strict about paying on time. No arrears.

IRMA: I never get in arrears. It's not always easy.

ANNE KATHERIN: It'll be OK in the autumn when I've started the job. I mean it's well paid but I'm going to be short in July and August.

IRMA: You can always try to get work. The restaurants . . .

ANNE KATHERIN: I didn't want to have to. I tried to make myself save something from the grant. Useless. Thing is I need a rest. All that studying, studying, then sitting the bloody exams. As though they're the most important thing in the world. Madness. I'm telling you, though, I'm not over the nervous stress of it yet.

IRMA: Maybe you shouldn't stay up so late.

ANNE KATHERIN: I know but you get talking. Anyway it's not that. It's accumulated exhaustion.

IRMA: I'm a little tired myself so if you'll excuse me.

ANNE KATHERIN: See you then.

ANNE KATHERIN *turns and races up the stairs.* IRMA *follows.*

Scene Two

IRMA *stands in the doorway of the sitting room in her apartment. She glances carefully round the room. She puts her bags down, crosses to the record player, picks up the usual record and plays it. Then she sits down, her hand over her eyes. After a few minutes* GEORGE *enters from the bedroom doorway.*

GEORGE: Curtains.

He stands stock still.

IRMA: What?

GEORGE: You forgot to draw the curtains.

IRMA *gets up, draws the curtains.* GEORGE *walks to his chair – a hard dining-room chair – and sits down. All his movements are very quiet and he never raises his voice. His clothes and his hairstyle are old fashioned.*

You should take more care. You've no reason to be that careless. You should be able to do it in your sleep by now. You shouldn't even have to think about it.

IRMA: I'm sorry.

GEORGE: Every night you've to come in, look around . . .

IRMA: I don't want to talk about it, do you want a cigarette?

GEORGE: I'm dying for a fag, you got any?

IRMA: You smoke too much.

GEORGE: Not much else to do.

IRMA: Please.

GEORGE: You got a headache, it's the heat. I know myself, this weather, it's because it's stuffy, there isn't the air –

IRMA: I haven't got a headache.

GEORGE: Boss been at you, has he? I'd give the old bastard a piece of my mind. 'Look here', I'd say, 'how am I to keep body and soul together on these wages? Answer me that. It's easy for you', I'd tell him –

IRMA: He just tells me to chat up the customers and that way I'd make extra. He's right about that, of course, I would.

GEORGE: You shouldn't have to if you don't want to.

IRMA: George, there's pie from the restaurant in that bag. (GEORGE *looks in one of the bags.*) No, not that one, the other.

GEORGE: And use a plate.

IRMA: What?

GEORGE: You always tell me to use a plate.

IRMA: Do I? Good.

GEORGE: Really hungry I am. I'll make you some coffee in a jiffy.

GEORGE *eats hungrily,* IRMA *doesn't look at him.*

You can talk while I'm eating.

IRMA: Talk about what? I just want to sit still.

GEORGE: That's not fair and you know it.

IRMA: Eat your pie.

GEORGE: I've eaten my pie. Tell you what I'll put on the kettle –

IRMA: – And make a nice cup of tea.

GEORGE: Don't you want coffee?

IRMA: Yes. Please.

He goes into the kitchen, puts on the kettle.

The trouble is –

GEORGE *reappears round the corner of the doorway. His finger to his lips.*

The trouble is I'm getting too

old to chat up customers.

GEORGE: You've kept your figure.

IRMA: Why should they bother when there's fresh looking young girls everywhere they turn their heads. I don't want even to talk with them. I'd use sign language if I could. She, of course, is good at the backchat but then she's a Berliner.

GEORGE: You don't need any great looks or a friendly manner if you're the boss's wife. Bitch. Though it's him I hate the worst.

IRMA: She's a good woman in her way. She never asks a question about anyone for instance. That's nice in a person. But then, about herself, she'd tell anyone anything. She has no discretion.

GEORGE: Discretion?

IRMA: I know what it means. Why couldn't you learn German? Too bloody lazy.

GEORGE: You shouldn't swear.

IRMA: Don't be ridiculous.

GEORGE: You shouldn't — it lowers you.

IRMA: My God.

GEORGE: Well it does.

He goes out and brings back a coffee pot, cups etc.

IRMA: Thank you George.

GEORGE: You were lucky to get such a good quality — remember that stuff . . .

IRMA: It's not so difficult to buy things as it was. I've told you that before.

GEORGE: You'll burn your lips if you gulp it down. Did you see any soldiers?

IRMA: Not this morning, you never really see them in the morning.

GEORGE: We were up at bleedin' dawn.

IRMA: I like that walk in the morning, going past the bakeries. What a beautiful smell, so refreshing, like being in another country.

GEORGE: Did you get any of it?

IRMA: No. Why should I when I can steal from the restaurant. So I get to work. The first to come are the drivers, one or two were drunk still. You would have pitied them having to drive hundreds of miles in such a condition. Then come the factory people, much more lively, telling jokes.

GEORGE: What kind of jokes?

IRMA: Günter, the one I told you about, he was there. He had everyone bent over laughing. His stories were crude of course. They're hard to translate as well but if you want — I was talking to Trudi —

GEORGE: Trudi?

IRMA: No, of course not Trudi. I forgot, no, I meant this new young woman who is working there now. She must remind me of Trudi.

GEORGE: I'd have thought he'd be too mean to take on new staff.

IRMA: A new face is good for business.

GEORGE: Well what's she like?

IRMA: Very talkative.

GEORGE: How tall?

IRMA: Hard to tell if a woman is wearing heels.

GEORGE: And young is she?

IRMA: She isn't from Berlin. She has the idea of becoming a teacher.

GEORGE: You didn't say her name.

IRMA: She talked about religion a lot.

GEORGE: What's her name?

IRMA: Anne Katherin.

GEORGE: That's pretty isn't it? Blonde or brunette?

IRMA: I'm not telling you.

GEORGE: What was on the menu?

IRMA: Nothing new.

GEORGE: Maybe the new girl, maybe she can cook.

IRMA: Yes maybe.

GEORGE: What happened after lunch?

IRMA: I washed up and listened to the wireless. Oh and I broke a cup. He talked as though it was an heirloom. No more wireless if it was going to make me careless. May I have more coffee now?

GEORGE: Pass us the cup then.

He refills her cup.

GEORGE: When did the soldiers come?

IRMA: They were later today.

GEORGE: Perhaps there'd been some trouble.

IRMA: Perhaps.

GEORGE: Were they Americans?

IRMA: Oh yes Americans. How much noise they make, twice as much as anyone else, talking and laughing. It's amazing their high spirits.

GEORGE: You should have seen the food they got. No wonder they're such big hulking fellows. I'd have been if I'd had grub like that all my life.

IRMA: No George. You have such delicate bones.

GEORGE: I'm wiry that's what I am. Best type for sticking to a job. These big chaps are good now for a quick effort, lifting something heavy, but for long hours you need another sort. They fag out in a couple of hours while your slow steady man's just getting the feel of it. There was this chap —

IRMA: — Ian

GEORGE: — from Scotland, he got billeted onto a farm up past the village. Now he was over six foot standing.

IRMA: You've read me that bit often.

GEORGE: Well see what happened to him.

IRMA: He got out of the army, didn't he? That's nothing to complain about.

GEORGE: Don't you want a cigarette? You've not been smoking much lately. The cigarettes are a lot better than they used to be.

IRMA: I don't notice.

GEORGE: Do you fancy a bit of music? I used to love a dance. I wasn't bad on a dance floor, nothing fancy, but I wasn't shy.

IRMA: It's noisy in the restaurant.

GEORGE: I'll fetch dinner then.

IRMA: There's no need to hurry. I'm not that hungry today.

GEOGE: There was a good bit of meat in that pie. The boss has good friends, I bet, on the black market.

IRMA: I got a can of coke and some chocolate.

GEORGE: Did you? Can I have them if you're not hungry?

IRMA: Why not. Look in the bag.

GEORGE: You're a good sort, Irma. From an American were they?

IRMA: Perhaps I reminded him of his mother, what do you think?

GEORGE: What's that?

IRMA: Perhaps I reminded the Yankee of his mother and that's why he gave me the can and the chocolate.

GEORGE: You don't look much like an American.

IRMA: What do I look like?

GEORGE: Very well, only a little tired maybe. Stands to reason if you've been on your feet all day. You've kept your looks, both of us have. Though I have to worry more about taking exercise.

IRMA: Do you know what today is?

GEORGE: Look at this.

He lies down and does a couple of press-ups and then he laughs.

There's life in me yet. All my family are famous long livers. My uncle George, he was my great uncle, now he lived to be over 87. He was 87 when I last saw him and hale and hearty as you like.

IRMA: It's an anniversary, you like things like anniversaries.

GEORGE: I made some soup, the Russian one you like. The one with beetroot.

IRMA: It's seven years to the day.

GEORGE: I'll fetch you some. It'll do you good you know.

He gets up and goes towards the kitchen.

IRMA: I'll wait till you get back. You needn't hurry.

GEORGE *re-enters with a soup bowl, bread etc on a tray.*

GEORGE: Sit up and eat it. You should sit up to eat otherwise you get your digestion cramped.

IRMA: And where is yours?

GEORGE: I've already had mine. You get hungry waiting.

IRMA: I'll eat it here.

GEORGE: You should sit up.

IRMA *holds out her hands and takes the tray.*

IRMA: I was telling you about an anniversary. Do you realise it's seven years to the day that you last made love to me? Why don't you fetch the book and read it to me while I'm eating. Did you write much today?

GEORGE: I don't really like this hot weather.

He gets up.

Did you lock the door?

IRMA: Yes of course.

GEORGE: Well you forgot the curtains when you came in.

IRMA: I remember.

GEORGE: It should be a matter of routine. You come in and turn on the hall light. You lock the front door. Bolt it. You check the door and then you pull over the curtain to keep the sound in. Then you come in here and see does the room look as it should. Then you draw the curtains over the window. Right over the windows. Without any gaps.

IRMA: I know this George.

GEORGE: Then you pick up the record, the right record and turn on the gramophone. When I hear the music I can come in. All it takes is one little slip, one careless –

IRMA: Why don't you fetch the book and read it to me. Please.

GEORGE: I don't want to have to say these things you know.

IRMA: Just remember to keep your voice down if you're going to lose your temper.

GEORGE: And then you get me angry. You don't listen. You don't take proper notice of me, you start teasing me so I could end up losing my temper and shouting. It'd be understandable if I did. It's not understandable forgetting the curtains.

He goes out of the room. IRMA drinks a little soup and crumbles the bread. GEORGE returns with his writing book. They are exercise books tied with string.

IRMA: Did you mend the light in my bedroom?

GEORGE: The whole place needs rewiring.

IRMA: You make a good soup.

GEORGE: The sort that mother used to make eh?

IRMA: Not mine.

GEORGE: There were people moving about today. I could hear them banging things. They didn't have voices I recognised. I meant to tell you first thing but the curtains put it out of my mind.

IRMA: Somebody came across some furniture and decided to buy it I expect. If you've money you can find anything.

GEORGE: I like our furniture.

IRMA: They're building new apartment blocks. Very tall and modern like New York.

GEORGE: It worried me. I was even wondering if someone had passed away and they were bringing out the coffin. Daft really but you never know. They'd have a reason then for coming round.

IRMA: Most people die in hospital.

GEORGE: Not if there was an accident. A fatal accident or worse. Something deliberate. It'd give the police an excuse then for checking all the flats out.

IRMA: They don't need excuses.

GEORGE: I'll read you an early bit, from the beginning of the war when I was still at home. I was eighteen, nearly.

He coughs and begins reading.

'The weather was beginning to get cold. We were saving on coal so I spent the morning chopping wood in the yard. It's an old axe and not very handy but Dad wouldn't hear of getting a new one. He was always against spending and now he talks on and on about the war effort just because it suits him. I have to wear Billy's old shirt which is too big and not warm. One of the sisters could knit me gloves which I've said often enough but they're a pack of lazy bitches. They do nothing all day but quarrel, especially in the kitchen. I never go in the kitchen except to eat — not even for the warm stove that gets lit because I chop the wood. One of them should clean that stove. All it needs is a bit of elbow grease. Mary's a little better than the other two. She reads me bits from the paper on the Sunday. She cooks the best as well, with the other two it's muck. We're lucky as well, rationing can't be as bad on a farm. There's less eggs and less butter. We've less butter because of losing most of the herd and ploughing up the grasslands. First time I saw Dad on a tractor I laughed till I hurt, he looked like fury. Less money in grain than cows he reckoned but you can't do nothing if the government say so. The inspectors are here nearly every week 'cos they don't trust him 'cos they've got more sense.

This particular day there'd been a lot of light in the sky the night before. I'd seen it because my window's towards the coast. I'd said about it at breakfast but Dad never talks till midday. It's like he's dazed; not in a bad humour, he just doesn't listen. Over dinner is when he's likely to fly off the handle at the least thing. All the good crockery my Mum brought has long gone, Jane says, but I don't remember it anyway.

I wondered if there'd been a big fire somewhere. We don't get the papers except the one on Sunday. Nobody calls and we don't go to the village much. The girls hadn't seen nothing but they sleep in the opposite direction and face Princetown if they face anywhere.

There's a lot of work on today, I
had more things to do than time to
do 'em. There's a lot I miss about
Billy having gone. My Dad is out in
the fields all morning. In the
afternoon I was trying to fix up the
fence but it's no use without good
strong wire which can't be had that
easy these days. In the old days
they built them with stone. I'd go
daft doing that, it's so slow.

I could see Dad up on the tractor.
He hates ploughing up that grass.
He won't let anyone else on it not
even me though I'd dearly like to
try it. He said to them the land was
wrong, too much clay but they just
told him if he couldn't manage
himself, someone would be sent
here. That shut him up quick, he
never likes a stranger.

I was starving by dinner time. I am
always. I hope Mary's been cook
and she had. She makes a nice stew
with a good thick gravy. I tell her
so and she looks pleased. After
there was a fruit pie but the pastry
was hard. Dad never notices what
he eats.

Anyway there I was with a
cigarette and my cider just settling in
front of the fire and Dad's asleep
nearly, when Uncle Charlie walks in.
Behind him trails his whole
bloomin' family, except the
daughter that's married and has a
job in the North — where, I don't
know.

The long and the short of it's this.
Last night the Germans had come
over Plymouth and bombed it half
way to hell, he said. He was on
leave. He'd been a merchant seaman
all his life. It was lucky he was on
leave he said otherwise what might
have happened. They'd hidden in
the cellar till the all clear. They'd
sung hymns said Nancy, laughing.
Soon as the all clear comes Uncle
Charlie packs up what he wants and
leaves it with a neighbour to be sent
on, and off he sets with the lot of

them following. He'd decided he
wouldn't rest till he'd found
somewhere safe for them to stay.
His leave was up at the end of the
week. He gave my Dad a look and
said that of course he'd thought of
him.

IRMA: Nancy.

GEORGE: I like reading about that
time. It's nice writing it too.

IRMA: Why, George?

GEORGE: I hated it even more later.

IRMA: The dirt, the sergeants shouting
at you, running with half a ton on
your back and those horrible
landmines.

GEORGE: They were horrible.

IRMA: Poor boy.

GEORGE: They were meant for tanks.
Once I saw four lads blown apart
quick as a wink.

IRMA: There were bits of them all
over you. Didn't you do any new
writing today?

GEORGE: There's always more of it.

IRMA: You have to carry on George.
Somebody might want to read it
one day.

GEORGE: It'd be a real help to me if
you could spell. I don't like to use a
word unless I know it's spelt right.

IRMA: I bought you a dictionary
twenty years ago.

GEORGE: I can't make head or tail of
it, half the words in it are bloody
foreign.

IRMA: I'm sorry.

Scene Three

MR HANUSSEN, *standing outside the
door of his flat, catches sight of*
ANNE KATHERIN.

MR HANUSSEN: Ah good, I've been

trying to catch you.

ANNE KATHERIN: Pardon?

MR HANUSSEN: You're the new tenant I believe. I've been hoping for an opportunity to introduce myself. My name is Mr Hanussen –

ANNE KATHERIN: Call me Anne Katherin.

MR HANUSSEN: Miss Anne Katherin – ?

ANNE KATHERIN: I don't like my surname, it's ridiculous.

MR HANUSSEN: I am by way of being the unofficial caretaker of this building. Strictly unofficial. That is to say, as the oldest resident – I mean the longest tenant – I do not refer to my age: I feel I have a certain responsibility. Any complaints or queries you might wish to raise with the landlord; I would be willing to act as go between. Often it's a thankless task. Ingratitude. I also feel it my duty, a far more pleasant one, to welcome new tenants to the house and offer sincerest wishes –

ANNE KATHERIN: I suppose the landlord's pretty strict about rent on time?

MR HANUSSEN: Naturally.

ANNE KATHERIN: I'd heard that.

MR HANUSSEN: Understandably in my opinion.

ANNE KATHERIN: How long have you lived here?

MR HANUSSEN: Seventeen very contented years.

ANNE KATHERIN: Then you're not the longest tenant.

MR HANUSSEN: I beg your pardon.

ANNE KATHERIN: I met a woman on the stairs the other day and she, for sure, has been here longer than seventeen years. And she had an honest face.

MR HANUSSEN: You are referring, I take it, to the woman inhabiting Flat 14?

ANNE KATHERIN: Yeah.

MR HANUSSEN: I was naturally referring to myself as the longest standing respectable tenant.

ANNE KATHERIN: She's not respectable?

MR HANUSSEN: I am not willing to discuss the matter further.

ANNE KATHERIN: Ah go on.

MR HANUSSEN: I am unable.

ANNE KATHERIN: Why?

MR HANUSSEN: I have a possibly old fashioned respect for both your youth and your sex.

ANNE KATHERIN: Sex?

MR HANUSSEN: I meant –

ANNE KATHERIN: You mean she's a whore? She does it for money? She fucks for money?

MR HANUSSEN: You're a student I take it?

ANNE KATHERIN: Not any more.

MR HANUSSEN: Expelled perhaps?

ANNE KATHERIN: I have my certificates upstairs – not that I'm offering to show them to you.

MR HANUSSEN: Allow me to give you a few words of warning.

ANNE KATHERIN: Not interested.

MR HANUSSEN: Step inside here please.

He goes into his flat. ANNE KATHERIN hesitates and then follows him.

MR HANUSSEN: I would offer you coffee but you probably prefer beer.

ANNE KATHERIN: Christ!

MR HANUSSEN: It would be a matter of pride to say you did anyway.

ANNE KATHERIN: What's all this china here for?

MR HANUSSEN: They are ornaments. Excuse me while I go to the refrigerator.

ANNE KATHERIN: Feel free. Are you a retailer?

MR HANUSSEN: Would you like a glass or would you enjoy it more straight from the bottle?

ANNE KATHERIN: There's a very lonely atmosphere in this room.

MR HANUSSEN: Indeed?

ANNE KATHERIN: Indeed and I'll have a glass please. All the china ornaments don't help. They make it look eerie. Do you sell them or what?

MR HANUSSEN: No I buy them.

ANNE KATHERIN: Are they supposed to be antiques? God they're ugly. I mean the colours are —

MR HANUSSEN: You find them vulgar?

ANNE KATHERIN: Still if you like them it's your business.

MR HANUSSEN: They're not here because I like them. They are of practical use so naturally I bought the cheapest available.

ANNE KATHERIN: Yeah?

MR HANUSSEN: Pay attention, I'm going to give you a little good advice.

ANNE KATHERIN: Look, I don't mind having a beer with you, I'm not busy —

MR HANUSSEN: The worst thing about your generation —

ANNE KATHERIN: Jesus.

MR HANUSSEN: — Aren't your ideals. Naturally I hate Communists but you aren't Communists, you're idiots.

ANNE KATHERIN: Change the record.

MR HANUSSEN: What record? I'm afraid I don't . . .

ANNE KATHERIN: Never mind, just get on with it.

MR HANUSSEN: The Communists at least are organised, you on the other hand are a rabble. This is a subject to which I have given a good deal of thought.

ANNE KATHERIN: Very kind of you but you needn't have bothered.

MR HANUSSEN: In the old days —

ANNE KATHERIN: Not the old days.

MR HANUSSEN: We may have been misguided but we knew what road we were travelling on. There were ideals. When we changed things, we changed the whole world, the entire course of history and why?

ANNE KATHERIN: Because you were mad, that's why.

MR HANUSSEN: Only a few were.

ANNE KATHERIN: I know this'll be a big surprise to you but I'm not actually interested in the war and all that crap.

MR HANUSSEN: I take it you've participated in the demonstrations against the Americans' war?

ANNE KATHERIN: None of your business.

MR HANUSSEN: Perhaps with a crash helmet on and a scarf round your face so that if your picture's in the paper it won't upset your family.

ANNE KATHERIN: It's more to do with keeping yourself off police files. They have hundreds of photographers on those things.

MR HANUSSEN: I forgot to offer you a cigarette.

ANNE KATHERIN: I'm trying not to smoke. It's bad to be dependent.

MR HANUSSEN: As I was saying, it's impossible to take you seriously. You've no courage, no guts.

ANNE KATHERIN: It's not just demos you know, people are taking other actions.

MR HANUSSEN: Such as?

ANNE KATHERIN: Well like burning up that department store. Hitting American bases. Taking on the whole State. I mean that's not chicken feed. It takes real courage to do that.

MR HANUSSEN: The terrorists, you mean them? You approve of them?

ANNE KATHERIN: I don't really want to get into this.

MR HANUSSEN: The other major thing that's lacking is a sense of vision. All you have is some half baked notion of what some Jew wrote back in the last century.

ANNE KATHERIN: So you're anti-Semitic as well? I should have guessed.

MR HANUSSEN: Nonsense, I support Israel.

ANNE KATHERIN: I have to be going.

MR HANUSSEN: You haven't finished your beer.

ANNE KATHERIN: You've a nerve to call us cowards. After the war, for ten, fifteen years there's not a peep out of you. Nobody talks about it, let's forget the whole unfortunate episode. Let's get back to normality, let's get rich and impress the whole world with our nice new Germany. When I was a kid, if I asked too many questions – upstairs to bed. Last time I was home he went on for five hours, five hours about it. And it's all crap: self-justification, the being led astray, not understanding – but Germany was in a real fix, the stab in the back, suitcases of money for

one lousy egg. He is like all of them caught between public shame and private justification for what happened. Hypocritical bastards.

MR HANUSSEN: At the time I was proud to join the army. I was glad to be sent to the Russian front, the real enemies were always the Communists. I wanted to join a panzer division. I should have, I'd done a year's apprenticeship as a mechanic. My father, a good man, placed me in the hands of a real craftsman, a genius with his hands.

ANNE KATHERIN: It must have been very chilly out there in Russia.

MR HANUSSEN: Everything kept seizing up, the guns, the engines – because of the cold.

ANNE KATHERIN: I suppose you got frost-bite.

MR HANUSSEN: I was wounded and got frost-bite waiting to get to the station. They had to cut the leg off.

ANNE KATHERIN: Well I'm sorry to hear that.

MR HANUSSEN: I was sent back to Berlin. The city was in chaos, everyone walking around with guns in their hands. We were all hungry. That's when I gave up smoking. Kept the cigarettes for barter. You could get anything with them – drink, food, women. There were raids all the time day and night. Who could stop them? The dust was everywhere all the time. I swallowed pounds of it, you could have sieved half the city through a tea strainer.

ANNE KATHERIN: Must have been hell for asthmatics.

MR HANUSSEN: I was trapped for eight hours in the rubble, trying not to breathe. I wanted so badly to be unconscious, I kept willing and willing myself. The raid hadn't been a heavy one and it wasn't even that nearby. It was just unfortunate that the walls of the houses couldn't take any more. They'd had enough and down they crashed. You can keep on dreaming of the same thing for years. A friend said to me — get a chandelier and string it up, you hear it moving unexpectedly, just race to leave, don't wait — just run. But where was I to find a chandelier? It would be madness to try and find out. So I reason it out: china, I think to myself, china is as sensitive as glass. What I need is to fill a shelf, pack them close as can be so that —

ANNE KATHERIN: Actually I would like a cigarette.

MR HANUSSEN: Pardon?

ANNE KATHERIN: Cigarette.

MR HANUSSEN: I think I do have a packet or two somewhere in case visitors were to drop in.

ANNE KATHERIN: It's OK. Don't bother looking, you could knock the ornaments off.

MR HANUSSEN: To continue then. I knew it would all be over soon. So I hid in a house not far from here until the Americans came. It was nothing to be ashamed of. It was a matter of self preservation when there was nothing else to preserve.

ANNE KATHERIN: You deserted?

MR HANUSSEN: Then we were taken to a POW camp —

ANNE KATHERIN: Do you mind if we leave it there? I don't think I could stand to hear about the turnip stew, the turnip jam etc. If you don't mind, let's drop it.

MR HANUSSEN: What would your parents say if they could hear you talking so rudely to an older man and a cripple?

ANNE KATHERIN: It's too depressing to think about. Will I fetch you another beer?

MR HANUSSEN: No thank you.

ANNE KATHERIN: Come, don't sulk. I tell you what, give us some more advice, you enjoyed that earlier.

MR HANUSSEN: I will not be cajoled.

ANNE KATHERIN: Or you could tell me about the despicable things Miss Hoffener gets up to in her flat.

MR HANUSSEN: I will say no more than that I am not deaf.

ANNE KATHERIN: What have you heard?

MR HANUSSEN: Footsteps, not female footsteps but male footsteps.

ANNE KATHERIN: She could have friends round.

MR HANUSSEN: She has no friends.

ANNE KATHERIN: How do you know?

MR HANUSSEN: You can hear them at all hours of the day and night. She is discreet, I'll grant her that, not once have I caught a suspicious character on the stairs. Besides which, what does she live on? She has no job and once I caught sight of her in a very insalubrious area of the city. Loitering on a pavement.

ANNE KATHERIN: What were you doing in this insalubrious area?

MR HANUSSEN: On a more personal level she has, in my view, a most shifty and evasive look about her. She is without doubt one of the most unsociable people in this whole block — in the entire street. You may rely on my judgement, that woman has something to hide.

ANNE KATHERIN: We probably all have.

MR HANUSSEN: What have you got to hide?

ANNE KATHERIN: Me? Nothing.

MR HANUSSEN: We've been warned

to keep an eye out for suspicious characters. Particularly if they're young student types.

ANNE KATHERIN: Don't be crazy, I've nothing to do with them.

MR HANUSSEN: With whom?

ANNE KATHERIN: I've a job starting as a teacher in the autumn.

MR HANUSSEN: You admitted going on the demonstrations.

ANNE KATHERIN: That's different.

MR HANUSSEN: Then you've nothing to be afraid of when the police do come to this building.

ANNE KATHERIN: No.

MR HANUSSEN: They will eventually. It used to be a real Communist stronghold this area, and now it's full of Turks and students. It's one of the first places they'll look. It doesn't really matter that this particular block looks and is respectable. I'm only warning you in a friendly way.

ANNE KATHERIN: I suppose I should thank you.

MR HANUSSEN: Yes you should.

ANNE KATHERIN: Thank you.

MR HANUSSEN: That's better, it costs nothing to be polite.

Scene Four

In the afternoon, Sunday, after dinner.

GEORGE: That was a lovely dinner, really lovely. Considering your wages we don't do too bad.

IRMA: It's the tips and, of course, what I can steal.

GEORGE: Shouldn't really steal you know.

IRMA: I like to see you eat.

GEORGE: Shall I have my bottle of beer or wait?

IRMA: Have a cigarette George — they're on the table.

GEORGE: I'll save it for a bit longer then.

IRMA: Wouldn't it be nice if we could go out for a walk?

GEORGE: Don't spoil things.

IRMA: We could stroll in the park and you could tell me the names of all the trees. I don't know their names in German even. There would be birds and beautiful fresh air. It would be so pleasant to walk arm in arm together and look at the statues and the flowers. How you would enjoy yourself.

GEORGE: Don't spoil it now.

IRMA: What's the harm in wishing for things? Even the condemned men are allowed a choice of breakfast.

GEORGE: Come on Irma.

IRMA: What's the matter?

GEORGE: You know what I mean.

IRMA: It would be nice.

GEORGE: It only makes matters worse.

IRMA: I think I'll go and lie down in the bedroom, I'm sick of sitting in here.

GEORGE: I'll put on some music, that'll cheer you up.

IRMA: Maybe I'd be better after a sleep.

GEORGE: What music do you fancy? I wish we had a wireless.

IRMA: I'm out at work all week.

GEORGE: Then put your feet up and relax. Why don't you open a window if you're stuffy? Better not though, sound has a way of travelling. If someone else has a window open we'll be overheard.

IRMA: I'm going for forty winks.

GEORGE: But you haven't read me

the paper yet.

IRMA: George —

GEORGE: Yes?

IRMA: Ah — what does it matter.

GEORGE: I like to listen to the paper on a Sunday. You know I like the paper on a Sunday.

IRMA: You only want to hear about the criminals, the murders and the rapes.

GEORGE: That's not true.

IRMA: Don't pretend.

GEORGE: That's not true and you know it. It's because you never bother —

IRMA: Perhaps I ate too much.

GEORGE: You hardly touched your dinner. I had to eat half your plate.

IRMA: Where is the paper anyway?

GEORGE: You were reading it in bed.

IRMA: Fetch it for me please.

GEORGE: You know I don't like walking about with the curtains open.

He goes into the bedroom and returns with the paper.

IRMA: You know the veins in my legs are like knots, they're so tight.

GEORGE: Here you are.

IRMA: It's not good for a woman my age to be standing all day. It affects the circulation.

GEORGE: This weather would get anyone down.

IRMA *takes the newspaper and reads it.* GEORGE *sits waiting.*

GEORGE: Come on then, I'm waiting.

IRMA: Nothing new, same stuff. Woman in Innsbruck cut to pieces in her back garden in the middle of the afternoon.

GEORGE: Dead?

IRMA: Nobody heard a thing but the brother-in-law's disappeared.

GEORGE: Terrible thing to happen.

IRMA *continues reading.*

What else is there?

IRMA: Oh you know.

GEORGE: Anything about home?

IRMA: This is a German newspaper. And besides, not much happens there. Very quiet and dull. It's not important any more except for the Yankees. They like the fact you speak their language. It's nice for them to go on holiday there.

GEORGE: They respected us. We stood alone. They only came in because the Japs caught them with their trousers down. They never had anyone like Churchill, he was a great man he was.

IRMA: He was a windbag. Who cares about him now? It's the Americans who call the shots.

GEORGE: I never understood much of all that, we voted Liberal and that was that. I was too young to vote anyway. Besides, it was a National Government then with everyone in it. Politics is a mugs game, my Dad said.

IRMA *puts down the paper and closes her eyes.*

Pity it doesn't have the cricket score. Used to love cricket. I was on the village team once or twice and I wasn't a bad all-rounder, though I say it myself.

IRMA: They play baseball now.

GEORGE: Not in England.

IRMA: I'm telling you, a lot's changed. You wouldn't recognise the place.

GEORGE: I'd probably hate it.

IRMA: I could sleep for a hundred years.

GEORGE: Still, I get homesick.

IRMA: I know.

GEORGE: It's not the same for you. You aren't even sure which country you were born in. My family, now, we've lived in that village —

IRMA: Shut up George.

GEORGE *picks up the newspaper.*

GEORGE: Who are all these, in the photographs?

IRMA: What?

He shows her the newspaper.

You can read the names yourself, they're printed underneath.

GEORGE: One of the girls is nice looking.

IRMA: Which?

She snatches the paper from him.

Nice looking? I can't see anyone here who's nice looking.

GEORGE: I didn't mean anything Irma.

IRMA: They all have crooked noses or crooked teeth.

GEORGE: I meant looked ordinary. You know, nice and ordinary.

IRMA: Ordinary? A fine judge of faces you are. I tell you, every last one of these is a killer. Oh yes even the pretty one here. Millions of pounds they've robbed, burnt —

GEORGE: They look very young for that kind of thing.

IRMA: They do it 'cos they don't like the Americans, but then who does?

GEORGE: I can't stick 'em. Still, they're young to be doing that kind of thing.

IRMA: Who cares how young they look.

GEORGE: Where would they get the experience, I mean someone would have to show them the ropes. Can't be that easy to rob a bank otherwise everyone would be at it. You'd need brains for that, planning all the details. The getaway's important and the hideout and then getting rid . . .

IRMA: They won't get away with it.

GEORGE: They might if they plan it well; think it all out beforehand.

IRMA: The police are after them. Their photographs are everywhere.

GEORGE: They'll never find them.

IRMA: They're searching every house in Berlin. They are bound to come across them, there's no doubt about it, no matter how well they've hidden themselves.

GEORGE: Searching every house?

IRMA: They're very dangerous people.

GEORGE: But then they'd be coming here.

IRMA: It's possible.

GEORGE: Why did you have to tell me you bitch.

IRMA: You asked, I answered. You wouldn't want me to lie.

GEORGE: You needn't have said —

IRMA: OK, they're not a fighting gang. No — far from it. In fact they are a sports team. A triumphant sports team returning home to receive applause and medals. Perhaps that's what they are and I was lying in the first place.

GEORGE: Were you?

IRMA: What?

GEORGE: You have to tell me.

IRMA: What?

GEORGE: Will there be house searches?

IRMA: How should I know.

GEORGE: It's been so peaceful for so long.

IRMA: For you perhaps, but just because you aren't there anymore doesn't mean the whole world has stopped.

GEORGE: What will we do?

IRMA: God this is a very drab-looking room. Look at the wallpaper. Wouldn't it be lovely if we could change everything in this room?

She gets up and goes to the window.

Come and look at the view from this window. No? Of course not, no. You shouldn't worry so much, suppose they do come, at least they'll be Americans and not bloody Germans.

GEORGE: You're getting over excited.

IRMA: Bloody Germans.

GEORGE: There's no need for language.

IRMA: Perhaps they won't be that thorough. I will talk to them charmingly. They'll offer me coke and cigarettes and nylons and chocolate. Perhaps they will. Perhaps they won't even go into the bedroom, let alone —

GEORGE: They'll have instructions. It'll be two to search each flat thoroughly and a third to question you. Then they'll report to the officer. If he gives a green light, they'll leave, but if he's the least bit suspicious he'll come himself. The first thing he'll say is, 'what's your name?'

IRMA: You should say it like an American.

GEORGE: I can't.

IRMA: Try.

GEORGE: What's your name?

IRMA: You're not trying.

GEORGE: What's your name, ma'am?

IRMA: Ah, that's good — 'ma'am', that sounds more like them. You

see, you can when you want to.

GEORGE: What's your name, ma'am?

IRMA: Miss Hoffener, Miss Irma Hoffener.

GEORGE: That's *Miss* Hoffener.

IRMA: That's correct.

GEORGE: And who lives with you, ma'am?

IRMA: I live alone sergeant. I've had this flat for over twenty years — ask the landlord, he'll tell you.

GEORGE: It's a large flat for one person, ma'am.

IRMA: I live here alone and always have.

GEORGE: You speak very good English.

IRMA: Thank you.

GEORGE: May I look at your ID card please.

IRMA: It's in my handbag.

GEORGE: I'd like to see it.

IRMA: I'm too tired to fetch it, George.

GEORGE: I'm not George, I'm the sergeant.

IRMA: I'm too tired whoever you are. Oh OK.

She goes into the bedroom, fetches her bag and gets her ID card.

Here you are.

GEORGE: Thank you, ma'am.

IRMA: Stop saying 'ma'am'.

GEORGE *looks closely at the ID card, turning it over etc.*

IRMA: You don't even know what a real ID card looks like.

GEORGE: Well, I'd notice if the inks were smudged or the letters weren't printed the same size. It's a very bad likeness of you.

IRMA: Do you know how much that

card cost me? For that price the ink is crystal clear.

GEORGE: You can tell it's a professional job.

IRMA: Give it back to me.

GEORGE: Do you think they will come round?

IRMA: How should I know.

GEORGE: It's not easy for me, I get frightened.

IRMA: Play some music and have your beer. Go ahead George, it will do you good.

Scene Five

GEORGE *and* IRMA *sit listening to the music. There is a knock on the door outside. For a brief second neither move. Then* GEORGE *picks up his knife, fork, plate and glass. He jams the cutlery into his pocket. The table now looks as though only one person has been eating. They both scan the room, then they both leave the room. There is a second knock. There's the muted sound of the toilet flushing.* IRMA *reappears. She goes to the doorway but doesn't open the door.*

IRMA: Who is it please?

ANNE KATHERIN: Hi, it's me.

IRMA: Who is that please?

ANNE KATHERIN: It's me, Anne Katherin. I met you the other day. I've just moved in. Look, it'll only take a minute but I have to see you.

IRMA: I'm not feeling well. I'm lying down resting.

ANNE KATHERIN: Just open the door for a second. I can hear you're standing in the hallway. I don't want to shout this all through the building.

IRMA: Perhaps if you were to push a note through the door.

ANNE KATHERIN: I get it, you've got company.

IRMA: No, of course I haven't. I live here by myself. This is a private flat.

ANNE KATHERIN: It'll only take a minute. Come on, don't be difficult. It won't do you any harm to talk to me.

IRMA: I'm sorry.

ANNE KATHERIN: What's the matter with you? For God's sake, if the place is in a mess I don't give a damn. What you do is your business. You shouldn't be embarrassed about it.

IRMA: Go away.

ANNE KATHERIN: I could always stay out here until you opened the door to come out you know.

IRMA *opens the door and turns back into the room,* ANNE KATHERIN *following.*

IRMA: There's nothing to see, now please –

ANNE KATHERIN: God it's really hot today isn't it? Really stifling. OK if I sit down? I've been running round the city all week trying to find a decent job. It's hard to be bothered with anything in this weather.

IRMA: I told you – a private apartment. Nothing to look at, nothing to see.

ANNE KATHERIN: All I got offered was crap. Maybe there's an opening in your line of work. What do you think, Irma, any chance?

IRMA: No, none whatever.

ANNE KATHERIN: You look a bit of a weird colour. You should open the windows or something. You look a bit yellow.

IRMA: I told you, I'm not well. I was resting –

ANNE KATHERIN: That guy downstairs doesn't like you much.

IRMA: Who? What do you mean? Which man? I was lying down resting and then suddenly in this girl barges.

ANNE KATHERIN: I didn't barge. I knocked. I never just tear into someone's room, never. This guy I know says you can tell this is a civilized country, even the police knock first.

IRMA: Why do you say that?

ANNE KATHERIN: It's supposed to be a joke – well not a joke exactly but more, you know, an ironic comment. You've probably forgotten my name, it's Anne Katherin.

IRMA: I try not to forget things.

ANNE KATHERIN: The guy I was talking about is the one living below you. Do you know him? Mr Hanussen. He's a bit weird. My God, I wouldn't trust him. His teeth must have cost a fortune. He should have spent his money getting his phoney accent polished up. Lecherous bastard. Every time he looked at my tits one of his hands twitched. Quite involuntarily. Pavlov's dogs. I'd say he's incredibly sexually frustrated. Probably having only one leg doesn't help. Though it's supposed to turn some people on. Each to their own taste. I don't want you to think I'm judgemental, not in that way.

IRMA: I may have passed him on the stairs.

ANNE KATHERIN: Well he doesn't like you, I can tell you that.

IRMA: But I've never spoken to him. Perhaps once or twice a comment on the weather, that's all.

ANNE KATHERIN: He's on his own, maybe he fancies you. He doesn't like to be ignored, he wants to talk his head off. Share his boring old experiences – Christ! I tell you this though, he's what I call a suspicious character. In both ways I mean. He's suspicious himself and he goes round suspecting others.

IRMA: Are you enjoying living in your new apartment?

ANNE KATHERIN: What? Oh yeah, well – I've one or two problems.

IRMA: The central heating isn't very good, but that doesn't matter much at this time of the year, does it?

ANNE KATHERIN: The main problem –

IRMA: All in all I manage well. It's comfortable here and you can feel safe.

ANNE KATHERIN: Unless they try throwing you out.

IRMA: I think I have a bottle of beer in the fridge.

ANNE KATHERIN: No thanks. The question is – if I don't get a job soon, how the hell am I going to pay the rent? It's impossible to ask my parents and totally pointless to ask any friends.

IRMA: How much do you need?

ANNE KATHERIN: A hundred or so. It's not even that much. I mean you think of the fat cats who'd blow more on one meal than I'd need for two months of my rent.

IRMA: I can only manage a hundred.

ANNE KATHERIN: Are you serious? I mean don't joke with me.

IRMA: That is all I can afford.

ANNE KATHERIN: You're really offering me a hundred? My God I was getting so worried – I was thinking of – never mind. Great, this is really marvellous.

There is a knock on the door.

Don't worry, I'll get it. You just sit

still and I'll tell them to go away.

IRMA: Please.

ANNE KATHERIN: Yeah who is it?

MR HANUSSEN (*from outside*): I trust I'm not intruding.

ANNE KATHERIN: You trust wrong.

MR HANUSSEN: Ah ha, I thought I caught a glimpse of you going into her flat. I've been out on a shopping expedition.

ANNE KATHERIN: Irma's not feeling too good, she's lying down. She doesn't want to be disturbed.

MR HANUSSEN: I take it she doesn't consider your presence a disturbance then? You are a newcomer, let me remind you.

ANNE KATHERIN: Don't be a pain.

MR HANUSSEN: I have a special bottle of schnapps with me. Listen.

He bangs the bottle against the door.

IRMA: Quiet, for God's sake be quiet.

MR HANUSSEN: People should be neighbourly, it's their duty. It's not good to live each one locked behind a door as though we are in separate confinement.

ANNE KATHERIN: It's solitary confinement.

IRMA: What does he want? What is he doing here? Isn't one enough?

ANNE KATHERIN: Give me a chance Irma, this guy's a gasbag, I told you that.

MR HANUSSEN: I can hear you talking. It's intolerable leaving me standing in the hallway with a door shut in my face. There's a word for people like you — anti-social. I'm talking to you Miss Hoffener and to you young lady.

ANNE KATHERIN: She's really not feeling well and needs a bit of quiet OK? Look I'll call down and see

you in a day or two.

ANNE KATHERIN *walks away from the door. MR HANUSSEN bangs the bottle again.*

MR HANUSSEN: It's the best stuff this.

ANNE KATHERIN: I think you should push off now Mr Hanussen.

MR HANUSSEN: Very well, I will return to my room. It is not my custom to intrude. Is a little respect so much to ask for? Oh yes, apparently yes. After all those sacrifices, not mine alone, I do not refer to mine alone. I was lucky to get back, to return at all. Even damaged, even missing one leg, even then I was privileged.

ANNE KATHERIN: He's off again.

MR HANUSSEN: You are a disgrace, a living shame both of you. The pair of you. I am not a fool, not an idiot. I can see what I can see. Don't ever doubt it, I beg you. You can't deceive me.

ANNE KATHERIN: Why don't you sleep it off?

MR HANUSSEN: As for you, have you ever thought of washing? Your hair is greasy, it's full of grease enough for a car engine.

Pause.

ANNE KATHERIN: I think he's gone.

IRMA: Yes I heard the floorboards creak. There's a loose one just before the stairway.

ANNE KATHERIN: See, I told you he was weird. He should be locked away, crazy old man. No I don't mean locked away. He wasn't as bad as that before.

IRMA: You'll want your money.

ANNE KATHERIN: Have you got it now? I can't get over it. Shows you how wrong you can be about people.

IRMA: Does it?

She goes over to the bedroom to collect the money.

ANNE KATHERIN: Yeah I mean I didn't think you were – you know – that friendly. I suppose I thought you were a bit stand-offish. Old people are always so quick to disapprove. I made the mistake of thinking you'd be like that.

IRMA *returns.*

IRMA: Here.

ANNE KATHERIN: Thanks. The minute things start going right – the autumn at the very positive latest . . .

IRMA: Goodbye then.

ANNE KATHERIN: Listen, it's a bit awkward this, after you've been so generous.

IRMA: There's something else you want.

ANNE KATHERIN: It's really why I called to see you.

IRMA: I'm listening.

ANNE KATHERIN: It's a mixture really. It's partly the old man and partly what you hear, newspapers and stuff, anyway I got worried.

IRMA: I don't understand.

ANNE KATHERIN: It's hard to know how to put it. I don't want you to misunderstand me. I'm not into violence. Quite the opposite. I mean I'm against war that's why I got involved. I suppose you know about Vietnam and what the Americans are doing there?

IRMA: I don't read that much.

ANNE KATHERIN: Loads of people are on our side – professors, doctors, lawyers. It's really only the government and they're just afraid of upsetting the Americans.

IRMA: A load of people dislike them.

ANNE KATHERIN: I was never involved in anything much. I went on the demos but everyone did. I didn't always hang out with the best people, OK that's true, but it's not a crime. Did I tell you I've a job as a teacher starting in the autumn?

IRMA: Yes.

ANNE KATHERIN: They check up on you, go through your file to see if you're a suitable person. I was all right, I got the job. I'd never joined anything you see. The only thing is, these fucking papers. They're not even mine, I promised this – friend – this friend's away at the moment you see. It's a small cardboard box about this big – just papers, leaflets, that kind of thing. Nothing really, but if the police were to call round it might look bad. I need that job you see. And that old man he might take it into his head to mention me to them.

IRMA: You want me to keep this box?

ANNE KATHERIN: Maybe I'm being silly. Do you think I'm being silly?

IRMA: You're very sensible not to want to get into trouble with the police.

ANNE KATHERIN: They said they were going to do a house to house search of the entire city. They really want to get them, it's like a vendetta. But they'll never manage, not the whole city, it would take forever.

IRMA: It would take time but if they want to do it they will.

ANNE KATHERIN: I bet a lot of people are getting nervous.

IRMA: Probably.

ANNE KATHERIN: There's lots of Turks and people –

IRMA: Go and fetch the box.

ANNE KATHERIN: Have you got

somewhere to hide it? I don't want —

IRMA: Go and fetch it.

Scene Six

IRMA *is sitting with the cardboard box full of papers in front of her.*

IRMA: There's nothing to be surprised at, it was bound to happen. It's only surprising that I'm surprised. It would be nice if this place was mine, if I lived here alone. I wish I could leave this city. I'd go to the East. I wouldn't care. Only to be somewhere different. I liked Poland. I could speak Polish once. He's sitting in the cupboard waiting for me to play the record. Wait then. I have to listen to your stupid boring book. Now it's my turn to talk.

I thought he was mad once — writing a book. Who would read it? Ah, he would, that's who, that's the important thing. Does he care if I listen? I wonder. I wondered, I couldn't care less now. He seemed so — safe, that was important then. Everyone was talking all the time or not talking at all. Running from place to place drinking everything they could find. Not him, he carried on as though, as though — I don't know. He seemed safe.

For years I'd been afraid. Every day it was possible they would take one look at my papers and then 'goodbye'. Bygones would be bygones. Every morning even before I opened my eyes I'd remember that. The thing to do was always to be pleasant and calm. Nerves are a private matter. I never guessed they would lose their war, not until nearly the last months. At the beginning I was relieved. I don't care. I don't care.

I had to survive. I was hungry all the time. Even before I was hungry. Some of them would pay with cigarettes. I had a job still. Trudi had been dead for eighteen months. She had been gone for eighteen months. It did her no good that she was a real German. It would have been worse, she told me that, to be Jewish. Or a gypsy.

My mother looked like neither. She was ugly that's all, but very strong. She would work and work. She's probably alive now somewhere. Still silent, just like a stone dropped out of the sky.

I must have fallen in love. There's no other explanation. George Coombe — what a nice boy he was, what lovely hands. I was tired — even then I was tired. I was worn out by frantic people living at their last gasp. His body was nice — it was even a little plump. The first present he gave me was a sheet. How kind I thought him. And soap as well. It was love. I liked everything about him even when we couldn't talk. He's so stupid at languages. That's what I can't understand. I wanted to be in bed with him all the time. I'd have slept with him anywhere. He was a nice boy and perhaps he could get me real papers.

He hasn't changed at all, not in the least. I have gone on getting older and older. I couldn't help that.

She gets up and puts on the record. After a pause GEORGE *enters.*

GEORGE: I'm here.

IRMA: Where else would you be?

GEORGE: I have to have a drink.

IRMA: Have one.

GEORGE: A real drink.

IRMA *passes him the key to the drinks cupboard. He pours her one and himself one.*

Tell me.

IRMA: It was just a girl. A new tenant. Nobody special.

GEORGE: I heard a man's voice.

IRMA: He stayed outside. I didn't let him in.

GEORGE: Have you locked the door? My God you haven't, have you? Well go and do it, you bloody bitch. What are you up to? Leaving the door like that, that's really smart that is. Very bloody sensible. I should knock you into next week.

IRMA *goes and locks the door. She returns and takes a sip of the drink.*

IRMA: Put the bottle away and give me the key please.

He obeys her.

GEORGE: I'm shaking with rage, look at me.

IRMA: There's nothing to worry about. You shouldn't get worked up. You might have heart failure and then what could I do?

GEORGE: Who was she?

IRMA: I told you the new tenant. You heard her things being moved in that week, remember? Her name's Anne Katherin, she's —

GEORGE: Anne Katherin?

IRMA: Yes that's right.

GEORGE: But that's the name of the new girl at work. You told me that that was the name of the new girl at work.

IRMA: Did I? It must be a coincidence then.

GEORGE: Why'd you let her in here? You mustn't ever do that. We made that a rule. First it starts by you forgetting the curtains and it ends with strangers coming into the place. We have to be careful — you know that.

IRMA: The first lover I ever had was called Paul.

GEORGE: Why are you doing this Irma?

IRMA: It was in Danzig. What a beautiful city. My mother was working but the pay was good at that time. We had a small attic to ourselves. I was supposed to be going to the hotels to find a job. I leaned over the bridge instead and looked down into the river. This young man approaches, very handsome. Perhaps he was handsome. He bowed and was very polite. Right away he started lying. He told me he was a count and very rich and that he loved me immediately. I turned to speak with him. Crap. I went with him without hesitation. Why, I wonder?

GEORGE: Nobody but you has crossed that threshold for twenty-seven years.

IRMA: Twenty-five.

GEORGE: It makes no sense.

IRMA: Why don't you read me a bit from that book of yours.

GEORGE: I'm not a self-pitying man you know that.

IRMA: Don't upset yourself George. Why don't we change the subject? There's a good boy.

GEORGE: I hardly ever complain. I did it for your sake, because you needed me.

IRMA: Not because you loved me.

GEORGE: That as well. I turned my back on everything.

IRMA: On what George?

GEORGE: On everything.

IRMA: You mean the happy homecoming? The family gathered to greet you, all welcoming smiles? I can read between the lines.

GEORGE: Slut.

IRMA: That still bother you? It never bothered me. I had to survive. Everyone else was doing the same. The men, the children. It didn't matter.

GEORGE: I liked the farm.

IRMA: The world has passed you by. You won't like it.

GEORGE: I never dream about firing squads now.

IRMA: What do you dream about?

GEORGE: Do you remember at first . . .

IRMA: I didn't dare sleep in case you woke up screaming and the neighbours heard. I held you all night. You have a very round head George.

GEORGE: If I'd have learned German would you have bought a wireless?

IRMA: Don't start that again. It's not good for you to get excited, look at how panicked you were about that girl.

GEORGE: I'm calm now.

IRMA: Good.

GEORGE: Irma, why did you let her in here? Who was she?

IRMA: She's blackmailing me.

GEORGE: Blackmailing you?

IRMA: That's right. She needs the rent you see and also she has some papers she wants hidden in case the police were to come. Do you want to look at them? They're under the table in that box.

GEORGE: She's in trouble with the police.

IRMA: She's not sure. It's not easy to be sure.

He begins looking at the papers.

GEORGE: How much money did she want? The bitch.

IRMA: I forget you can't read.

She takes a leaflet from him.

This is telling everyone that the Americans are shits and that we're

full of shit as well. Therefore –

GEORGE: What?

IRMA: We should smash the whole lot up from top to bottom.

GEORGE: She'll be back for more. Wait and see.

IRMA: The police they call pigs and bulls.

GEORGE: What'll we do?

IRMA: It's hard to imagine.

GEORGE: We have to plan.

IRMA: You have no identity card. I'd not get out of the city with mine. You don't speak German. How are we to leave Berlin, over there is the Wall and that side are check points. If we got to West Germany, what next? England perhaps? With no passports and no explanations. Everyone you remember will be dead or gone.

GEORGE: They'd shoot me.

IRMA: After all these years perhaps it would just be prison.

GEORGE: You don't know them.

IRMA: It doesn't agree with me this stuff.

GEORGE: I'll have it if you like.

IRMA: No.

GEORGE: Two drinks won't kill me.

IRMA: You're not used to it. It could make you loud.

GEORGE: Please, Irma.

IRMA: It's your life.

He drinks.

GEORGE: Did you say she was pretty?

IRMA: No I didn't.

GEORGE: We've stuck it out haven't we? Ups and downs and all. Shame for you about the kids.

IRMA: What kids?

GEORGE: That we didn't have any kids. Too late now.

IRMA: What's my age to do with it? You haven't made love for years.

GEORGE: Seven.

IRMA: Longer.

GEORGE: You said yourself seven.

IRMA: I did not.

GEORGE: Yes you did, the other week.

IRMA: I never once in my life said seven. That is a fact.

GEORGE: You did.

IRMA: Why have you always thought that anyway? That I wanted children? How many times have I ever mentioned wanting any? I wanted other things more.

GEORGE: You did say seven.

IRMA: What does it matter to you? You just enjoy being stubborn.

GEORGE: Is she really blackmailing you?

IRMA: Why should I lie?

GEORGE: Irma, you haven't said what we're going to do.

IRMA: Nothing.

GEORGE: We can't afford it. Look at the rent on this place. She'll want more — you mark my words.

IRMA: That's true.

GEORGE: And you'll just give it to her? How could she have found out, that's what I want to know. You must have been behaving suspiciously. Something must have given her the clue. What? That's what I want to know. Did you say something careless?

IRMA: I said nothing.

GEORGE: You left the curtains open with the lights on.

IRMA: Perhaps I'm losing interest.

Scene Seven

GEORGE *sits reading from his book.* IRMA *sits rolling cigarette after cigarette and putting them into a cigarette packet.*

GEORGE: The day I got my call-up papers you could have knocked me down with a feather. Never was so surprised in all my life. I had to sit down fast from the shock. Of course I thought being a farmer's boy I wasn't due to go into the army, not unless they actually landed. I'd know it would be official because of the envelope. I'm in a daze all day. I don't know what I did that day. It was the shock. When evening comes I walk across the back field for dinner as always. I wait till he's eaten, it's best to do that. Then I hand him over the letter. He reads it. All the girls are staring at me and looking at him. I don't get many letters. He must have read it over twice. He folds it up and puts it in his pocket. He doesn't say a word, only shrugs. I go upstairs and I'm shaking all over.

He turns over the pages.

They never give it a rest, not even on Sundays, because of church parade. All the time shouting and cursing. The language they use at you is very downright. Our sergeant swears at you steadily whether you're in the right or in the wrong. He comes right up to you when you're in the middle of doing something and starts screaming top blast in your ear. Of course it makes you doubt things.

He turns a page.

I'm in blisters from the boots. I greased them every night if I wasn't too tired but it didn't do them much good. All the others complain too. Perce puts his feet in meths to harden them up he says.

He turns back.

. . . just after Ma died, that very same winter. I wasn't home at Christmas that year — being the youngest I was at my uncle's in Plymouth. I didn't mind. My uncle bought me a telescope but I was to let the girls look through it. My aunt was good at puddings. She would say there was a real art to steam puddings. She put plenty of jam on it as well. After a while it was time to go home. It was cold that winter.

He turns forward.

It wasn't till the Yanks came that there was any trouble. They'd drunk anything. They pour spirits into their beer. The beer was mostly water. Perce used to call it piss but Eddie said there was more strength to piss than there was to this stuff. I think there wasn't enough hops. I prefer cider but I got used to it. There were terrible fights. There'd be our policemen and their policemen pulling us apart. The Yanks had more money than sense. They were always boasting. Nobody likes that. A lot of the girls went out with them because of the stockings, cigarettes and candy. Candy is the same as sweets to us.

He flicks forward, reading bits here and there.

. . . sitting in this French wood for weeks with nothing to do . . . myself, only I never got the chance . . . by the time the lorry came it was over. The wheels churned up a lot of stuff not just mud . . . in a potato field all night. There was never harder nor colder ground in the world. I was shivering going to sleep and woke up that way. Under my nails was nearly blue . . . the tea was hot. I kept my hands round the mug. Eddie hung his face over the mug and got his glasses misted. We all laughed . . . my feet were near crippled. I knew the blisters must be burst and bleeding. My socks were wet for one thing. Then my legs started aching. They were one mass of cramp but we're not allowed to stop. The pack was a ton weight too. Some of the lads began dropping in ditches when the sergeants weren't looking. But most times they were and they'd order you back to fetch it . . . a bridge with hundreds of tanks . . . not a soul left, dead or gone . . . the tower we blew to bits . . . crawling in the seams of your trousers. Some tried soaking the trousers in paraffin but that stank so bad . . . a lot of kids in the rubble, it must have been a school or something . . . finding a crate of beer down in the cellar . . . good night's sleep in ages. I lay there next morning smoking my cigarette. I'm always starving hungry first thing . . . sick to the teeth of all these ruins . . . Nobody understands a word of their lingo but the kids are learning ours fast enough. They were very smart the kids. It was a big city — you could see that even now. Eddie says it's half the size of London . . . The cooks are complaining about the food they're given to cook. The milk's blue looking 'cos of all the water put in it . . . all night. I even sang 'cos I was so drunk I didn't care that my voice is like a crow's. He wouldn't let me sing in the church even.

His voice fades out. IRMA *lights up a cigarette.*

Scene Eight

IRMA *sits on the stairs, she has a bottle of schnapps with her. She has been crying. Inside* ANNE KATHERIN's *flat* MR HANUSSEN *is talking.*

MR HANUSSEN: The institutions that bind a society together have to be respected.

ANNE KATHERIN: OK but why are you wearing a suit like that in this weather. At your age you should worry about your blood pressure.

MR HANUSSEN: You shouldn't sit there with a shirt half fastened – it looks vulgar.

ANNE KATHERIN: Shut up.

MR HANUSSEN: Do you know I was reading a most interesting thing the other day. Do you realise how many Russians are at this moment rolling over our heads in satellites and spaceships? Nearly twice as many as there are Americans. Now my view is –

ANNE KATHERIN: Vietnam's an expensive business. They have this stuff you see, you spray it from helicopters and the whole goddam jungle just rots away. Forever. Like a total desert. That must have cost a lot to develop.

MR HANUSSEN: If I were a young man that's what I would dedicate myself to, that would be my goal. In my opinion space travel is the most stupendous adventure undertaken by mankind.

ANNE KATHERIN: I wish to God these places were air conditioned or even ventilated properly.

IRMA *gets up and approaches the door of* ANNE KATHERIN's *flat. She hesitates.*

MR HANUSSEN: You mark my words because you'll live to see it. I won't of course. I'll be long dead and gone. Pushing up the daisies as the expression goes.

ANNE KATHERIN: What?

IRMA *goes back to the stairs, she takes a swallow of the schnapps.*

MR HANUSSEN: I've seen pictures of it. Not photographs of course but what they call artists' impressions. There on the moon – hundreds of new cities under gigantic plastic domes, reinforced naturally. Thousands and thousands of people will live and work up there. Children, new generations actually born on a different planet and that's only the start.

ANNE KATHERIN: What about the Martians?

MR HANUSSEN: I beg your pardon.

ANNE KATHERIN: I said what about the Martians?

MR HANUSSEN: I was talking about the moon.

ANNE KATHERIN: I suppose if there are any Martians we'll just blow them to bits. Or we'll put them into fucking zoos or we'll make them work for us on starvation wages. At the same time we'll tell them we're bringing civilisation to their backward planet. I can just see it.

MR HANUSSEN: There would be a benevolent policy. Do you have to express your opinions so crudely?

ANNE KATHERIN: Of course, there's always the hope that they're ahead of us and we'll be the ones colonised. That would be real justice. They'd pick Europe and America to settle in as we've got the industry and the expertise. Wouldn't it be great for once to see the robbers robbed?

MR HANUSSEN: Your attitudes are totally unnatural. You're hysterical. You should see a doctor, a brain doctor, someone who can –

IRMA *gets up and knocks on the door.*

IRMA: It's me. It's me.

ANNE KATHERIN: Hold on a sec.

MR HANUSSEN: Is it that person?

ANNE KATHERIN: Where are my bloody shoes?

MR HANUSSEN: As far as I'm aware you've not been wearing any.

ANNE KATHERIN: Oh yeah.

She goes and opens the door.
IRMA *enters.*

IRMA: I thought it wouldn't do me any harm to come and see you. I've schnapps here if you'd like a drink. I've been having a little celebration — you've company.

MR HANUSSEN: Mr Hanussen at your service.

IRMA: I can't shake hands.

MR HANUSSEN: It's a pleasure, a very distinct pleasure, to meet you Miss Hoffener.

IRMA: I'm disturbing you. I'd better go.

MR HANUSSEN: Especially after so many years. Seventeen I believe.

IRMA: I never said seventeen. I never once in my life said seventeen.

MR HANUSSEN: It's quite remarkable that we have lived in the same building for some seventeen years without conversing.

IRMA: What does it matter to you?

MR HANUSSEN: And now at last here we are having a civilised —

ANNE KATHERIN: Shall I get some glasses?

IRMA: Why not?

MR HANUSSEN: It's my personal opinion that neighbours have a social obligation and duty. Thank you, I will.

ANNE KATHERIN: I thought you'd prefer whisky.

MR HANUSSEN: Why would you think that? As I was saying, otherwise we may as well be barbarians and savages. Social intercourse —

IRMA: You haven't washed these glasses very well. Look at the rims.

ANNE KATHERIN: I've better things to do with my life than wash dishes all the time.

IRMA: It's not as though this stuff doesn't make me sick anyway.

MR HANUSSEN: We were in the process of discussing quite an interesting topic. What are your views on space travel, Miss Hoffener?

IRMA: I have no views.

ANNE KATHERIN: It does make more sense to drink beer in weather like this.

MR HANUSSEN: I would have thought that a woman in your line of work would have ample opportunity to become acquainted with the night sky.

IRMA: What does he mean?

ANNE KATHERIN: Ignore him.

IRMA: I want to know what he means.

ANNE KATHERIN: He thinks, or he says he thinks, that you make your living by being — by being a companion.

IRMA: A companion?

MR HANUSSEN: And here I am drinking ill-gotten gains. Very pleasant it is too, my dear.

ANNE KATHERIN: You're a malicious old fool.

MR HANUSSEN: And you are a half-baked Communist —

ANNE KATHERIN: Fascist, decrepit old fascist.

MR HANUSSEN: How dare you raise your voice to me.

IRMA: Don't raise your voice, people will hear.

MR HANUSSEN: Impudent –

ANNE KATHERIN: Impotent.

IRMA: You mustn't shout. What about the neighbours, what if they could hear?

MR HANUSSEN: I have nothing to be ashamed of, nothing to hide.

IRMA: If they caught you, a prison or the firing squad.

MR HANUSSEN: What does she mean?

IRMA: After all this time, how many years?

ANNE KATHERIN: Since what, Irma?

IRMA: The war of course, you remember the war.

ANNE KATHERIN: Not you as well Irma. I mean for God's sake, can't we talk about what's happening now? I mean it was over –

MR HANUSSEN: Twenty-five years ago.

IRMA: Perhaps they won't shoot you now.

ANNE KATHERIN: I think she's pretty gone on the drink.

IRMA: What's the difference if they put you in prison.

MR HANUSSEN: I have no idea of what you are trying to imply. Thousands were doing the same, besides which my position was regularised when I was a POW. I panicked, I explained to him, I didn't know what I was doing –

IRMA: That will convince nobody, don't be a fool. It's not your fault. You were born one.

MR HANUSSEN: I beg your pardon?

ANNE KATHERIN: How much of this stuff have you drunk, Irma?

IRMA: It shouldn't burn like this, not when it was so expensive. It was expensive. Why is he sitting like that?

ANNE KATHERIN: Like what?

IRMA: With his leg stuck out.

ANNE KATHERIN: You ask him, I'm sure he'd love to tell you.

IRMA: Why are you sitting there with your leg stuck out?

MR HANUSSEN: Wounds and frostbite on the Russian front. Conditions were appalling, they had to operate . . .

IRMA: Liar.

MR HANUSSEN: – There and then before the gangrene set in. I was lucky that they still had anaesthetics. Some poor devils after us . . .

IRMA: You stinking bloody liar. You weren't wounded – never, never, never. You spent all your time in potato patches and rubble. Haven't I heard you enough?

MR HANUSSEN: And for what did we suffer and die? So sluts like you could give yourselves to any Yank or Commie who offered you a couple of cigarettes.

IRMA: Why not? I had to survive. Everyone did, the men, the children. It didn't matter. They could take what they wanted anyway. If you got something from them, cigarettes, food, it kept you alive.

She drinks.

MR HANUSSEN: I don't think you should be listening to this kind of talk.

ANNE KATHERIN: It sounds pretty interesting to me.

MR HANUSSEN: If you had any self-respect you wouldn't remain here, Miss Hoffener. You would return to your room. There's nothing more unsightly than a drunken older woman – particularly of your type.

ANNE KATHERIN: Don't listen to him, this is my room. You stay as long as you want. Listen Mr Hanussen, I'd really prefer if you left now. I don't like the way you talk to Irma.

MR HANUSSEN: You are behaving in a very naïve fashion.

ANNE KATHERIN: OK.

MR HANUSSEN: Well, I am a little tired.

ANNE KATHERIN: I'll see you soon.

MR HANUSSEN (*whispering to* ANNE KATHERIN): If she tells you anything. If you get any more details. You will tell me, won't you? You promise?

ANNE KATHERIN: Yeah.

MR HANUSSEN: Good evening then – to both of you.

MR HANUSSEN *leaves.*

ANNE KATHERIN: Well, we really showed him off! Poor old sod. God he's so boring and pathetic. I'd blow my brains out before I'd end up like that.

IRMA: I knew he wasn't George because he doesn't look the same at all.

ANNE KATHERIN: Never told me his first name, that would be far too casual. He gives you the creeps in a way, doesn't he? I don't mean because he's a lecherous old idiot. It's just he's like a fucking fossil, nothing's really happened to him since the war. You should have heard him going on about space travel before you came. He's obviously read some crappy article, one with pictures, and was busy spouting away about it. Pretending he's modern. He's the kind who doesn't

know anything unless he reads it – and you can imagine the fascist crap he reads. You haven't got a cigarette?

IRMA: No smoking.

ANNE KATHERIN: I'd offer you some coffee, it'd do you good, except I haven't any left.

IRMA: No more money.

ANNE KATHERIN: Yeah that's right. I wanted to save that rent money. Once you start dipping in it'll disappear like smoke.

IRMA: Do I appear drunk?

ANNE KATHERIN: Well, not that bad. I mean you aren't staggering about or slurring, but you could probably do with some coffee. Do you mind if I go down and get some from your kitchen?

IRMA: No snooping.

ANNE KATHERIN: You shouldn't be paranoid.

IRMA: What's paranoid?

ANNE KATHERIN: It's when you think everyone's against you, plotting against you. That kind of stuff.

IRMA: That's fine then, I'm not paranoid.

ANNE KATHERIN: I'd better get you some coffee, really. You don't look well.

IRMA: No snooping.

ANNE KATHERIN: OK. I won't go down to your place, I'll run to the shop and get some there.

IRMA: No money.

ANNE KATHERIN: Fuck!

IRMA: You shouldn't swear, it always demeans you. He always says that every bloody time I swear.

ANNE KATHERIN: Men are like that.

IRMA: English men are even more

like that.

ANNE KATHERIN: Yeah? I wouldn't know. Look, I've enough for a small packet. Will you stay here while I go and get it?

IRMA: I'm not supposed to drink it.

ANNE KATHERIN: Coffee? That's crazy — coffee's good for you. There have been times in my life which I'd never have got through without coffee. Can't study without it for a start.

IRMA: You're a teacher.

ANNE KATHERIN: Yeah, that's right.

IRMA: Teachers teach, they don't study. You need to get your story straight.

ANNE KATHERIN: Really, I shouldn't drink any more, Irma.

IRMA: Where's the bathroom then?

ANNE KATHERIN: Just go through —

IRMA: It's the same layout as our place, isn't it? Poor old flat having the same layout as ours. While I'm gone, read this and tell me what you think.

She hands over her ID to ANNE KATHERIN *and leaves.* ANNE KATHERIN *looks at it, puzzled, and puts it down.* IRMA *re-enters the room and does the routine, closing curtains, locking doors etc. She sits down and laughs.*

Where's the music?

ANNE KATHERIN: What music?

IRMA *hums the tune she plays for* GEORGE.

IRMA: All young people are crazy for music.

ANNE KATHERIN: Look I can see you're not feeling well —

IRMA: Can you?

ANNE KATHERIN: It makes me nervous you locking the doors.

IRMA: There's nothing to stop you getting up, unlocking the door, turning down the handle, opening the door, walking out and along the corridor, down the stairs and —

ANNE KATHERIN: It's not that. I was planning to stay in this afternoon anyway.

IRMA: Nervous of going out? Scared the police will stop you?

ANNE KATHERIN: No, nothing like that. I had a late night that's all. I've a bit of a hangover if you want to know. Don't get that idea about me. I was probably being really stupid leaving that box of papers with you. It's just you can't open the papers at the moment without hearing about terrorists and everything. Then the old man was a bit — you know, sinister. That's all, it was just paranoia.

IRMA: I read some of them, the leaflets.

ANNE KATHERIN: What did you think of them? I know some people get put off by the jargon —

IRMA: You have too many books in one room. You should leave a window open regularly. Books make a place smell musty. I hate them myself.

ANNE KATHERIN: I have got a lot of them, you're right there.

IRMA: Do you know what surprises me about you?

ANNE KATHERIN: No, what?

IRMA: You wouldn't really want to hear.

ANNE KATHERIN: Yes I would, go on.

IRMA: No.

ANNE KATHERIN: I knew from the minute that we met on the stairs, I knew we'd get on.

IRMA: Well what surprises me about

you, is that you haven't asked for more money yet.

ANNE KATHERIN: What the hell do you mean by that?

IRMA: She thinks I'm being rude. That's ridiculous, you know.

ANNE KATHERIN: Listen you offered —

IRMA: I can be as rude as I like, it's none of your bloody business. What I want to know is, did you read the letter?

ANNE KATHERIN: What letter? I think you should go and lie down and get some sleep. You'll feel better. Jesus Christ, you try and be friendly.

IRMA: You tried to be friendly and then what?

ANNE KATHERIN: Nothing.

IRMA: I want to talk about the letter.

ANNE KATHERIN: Listen, I've never once touched anything of yours. I don't know anything about a letter.

IRMA: I gave you a letter when I went to the bathroom.

ANNE KATHERIN: You gave me your ID card when you went to the bathroom. God knows why.

IRMA: Well hurry up and read the letter.

IRMA *hands over the letter.* ANNE KATHERIN *begins to read it.*

ANNE KATHERIN: I don't understand.

IRMA: That's an unusual admission from you, Trudi.

ANNE KATHERIN: My name's not Trudi.

IRMA: I know what your damn name is, thank you. Is it a crime to call you Trudi? You don't look anything like her either. She wasn't always fidgeting and interrupting. She was a proper Communist as well when she was alive. When you're dead, you're dead, that was her view.

ANNE KATHERIN: I agree with that.

IRMA: She worked hard and she never blackmailed me.

ANNE KATHERIN: My God are you implying — you must be crazy.

IRMA: So I'll call you Trudi if I want to.

ANNE KATHERIN: I don't mind what you call me. Call me anything you like.

IRMA: So you're Trudi then. Well you and I, you and I are working. We've both jobs in a restaurant, a cafe really. I'm in the kitchen mostly washing dishes. You're nicer to look at so you're a waitress. You hate it. The food is — but you must remember the food. You couldn't buy real coffee then. Still it's always crowded. We hate the boss, both of us. If we ask for wages, he says we chat up the customers. We know what it means of course. He knows about us, that neither wants trouble. He has us eating out of his hand. Do you remember smuggling out those potatoes? Green as grass they were. You hid them in your knickers. We laughed and laughed. You never met George did you?

ANNE KATHERIN: No I don't think so. Did I?

IRMA: No, you were dead then.

ANNE KATHERIN: How did I die?

IRMA: In a camp of course. You were lucky to have stayed alive that long.

ANNE KATHERIN: Which camp?

IRMA: Who cares? Maybe you would have liked him, maybe not. If you had boyfriends you never talked about them. You were discreet. We fell in love, or I fell in love, maybe he did as well. Maybe it wasn't love at all. Maybe I just liked to sleep with him, does that shock you?

ANNE KATHERIN: No, of course not.

IRMA: Well, you've changed Trudi. You used to hate any talk about it. You were very serious, you liked me because you thought I was serious too. I wasn't of course, I was just afraid all the time. All the time I was afraid. Why didn't they come into the kitchen the day they came for you? I stood there my arms in the water trying not to scream or cry. My papers – but I showed you my papers. They're good aren't they?

ANNE KATHERIN: What? I'm not following this.

IRMA: Did you like my ID card?

ANNE KATHERIN: Yeah, as much as you can like ID cards.

IRMA: I'm talking to you about George, you should be listening. He was a soldier, every man in the world was then. He wasn't in the first, he was in the second or third wave to reach Berlin. Things were more relaxed, we'd got used to the situation. There was even a little more to eat – for some that is. He hated the army, he hated Berlin and he hated the idea of going home. Hate isn't the right word at all. I can't remember how we decided, if we did decide – which ever way it happened he wasn't going back.

ANNE KATHERIN: So what happened in the end?

IRMA: I never got to the end.

ANNE KATHERIN: You didn't report him, did you?

IRMA: To who?

ANNE KATHERIN: I don't know, whatever authorities were around then.

IRMA: Are you crazy? I don't report people to authorities. I've got myself to consider for a start. Really, Trudi, you're asking the strangest questions.

ANNE KATHERIN: I'm sorry.

IRMA: We carried on. After the war there was the blockade then the fuss about the Wall. So what, I said to myself, so what? And between us, if it wasn't good by then, it wasn't bad. He didn't care about much, not really, he just wanted to write that book. Do you know that that was my idea? It kept him quiet, it kept him quiet. That was the important thing – if the neighbours got suspicious. What would you have done Trudi?

ANNE KATHERIN: I – I don't know. Irma, I'm not sure I'm understanding this.

IRMA: Of course it couldn't go on forever. Not forever – it was always a matter of time. That's what I want to explain. Poor George.

ANNE KATHERIN: Where is he now?

IRMA: Now? In his little cupboard that we built so very very quietly. There's a light and ventilator holes. Maybe he's lying on the bed. My bed.

ANNE KATHERIN: Are you serious?

IRMA: You see, it's easy to repeat the same mistakes. There you go again Trudi asking me if I'm serious.

ANNE KATHERIN: This George character is still here, is that what you're saying?

IRMA: He had no choice once he'd deserted.

ANNE KATHERIN: My bloody God.

IRMA: It's been a long time.

ANNE KATHERIN: A long time!

IRMA: But I always knew it couldn't go on for ever.

ANNE KATHERIN: I can't decide if I think you're crazy or what.

IRMA: You knew. You knew I had

something to hide, you wanted to know what. You were curious, perhaps you could turn it to your advantage. Why else were you talking to me?

ANNE KATHERIN: Look maybe I thought — it doesn't matter what I thought. I didn't suspect any of this, it's not the kind of thing anyone would imagine.

IRMA: You're right, I don't need to pretend you're Trudi. I don't care about it, you're welcome to the money. It doesn't matter. I've enough to get me into the hospital if I decide to go. I can't make up my mind. I suppose it depends on the pain. That's the one thing that's hard to endure when it's physical.

ANNE KATHERIN: That's what the letter's about.

IRMA: You're supposed to read things fluently. How will you impress people otherwise? You're not going to be a success as a teacher.

ANNE KATHERIN: What is it? What have you got?

IRMA: Cancer.

ANNE KATHERIN: My grandmother died of it. It's horrible. I'm sorry.

IRMA: So when you get inside my flat you go into the room and lock the door behind you, walk over and draw the curtains. Then you put the record on the turntable and switch it on. He'll come out in a few minutes.

ANNE KATHERIN: I don't want to meet him.

IRMA: He wants to meet you. He's curious as well, sometimes. I can't remember what I said about you. Probably lies, I lie to him a lot.

ANNE KATHERIN: You haven't got a cigarette have you?

IRMA: He'll be shocked of course, but

he's robust, he won't faint. He hasn't seen anyone else but me in all these years. He'll think you very beautiful. I don't want you to sleep with him.

ANNE KATHERIN: Sleep with him!

IRMA: Why should he when he won't sleep with me. You tell him exactly what I tell you to. Show him the letter if you like. You'll have to translate.

ANNE KATHERIN: I'm not getting involved in this, there's no chance of it.

IRMA: Oh you have to.

ANNE KATHERIN: No I don't. He's nothing to do with me. He's your responsibility.

IRMA: No he's not. Not any more. It's my right to be on my own before I die. It's only humane.

ANNE KATHERIN: What are you going to do?

IRMA: I'm not decided. I wouldn't tell you if I was. I'm going to leave by the front door and disappear into thin air.

ANNE KATHERIN: You're just going to walk out explaining nothing, not even saying goodbye to someone you've been living with all those years?

IRMA: He'll panic but after that's over he'll be all right. He's not good at making decisions, you'll have to help him.

ANNE KATHERIN: What decisions?

IRMA: Well he'll either have to give himself up or decide to carry on in hiding.

ANNE KATHERIN: If you're not there . . .

IRMA: He's a nice man, you might like him. He needs to exercise, in case he gets fat. He's too fond of sweet things. He's very greedy. And

boring of course, but you could
educate him if you like. You could
teach him German for one thing. I
never could. You do speak English,
of course?

ANNE KATHERIN: Not that well.

IRMA: You'll improve, I did.

ANNE KATHERIN: Are you seriously
suggesting handing over this guy for
me to keep? I can tell you that
there isn't any possibility —

IRMA: It's your choice. You can do
what you like with him. All I'm
asking you to do is to tell him that
I'm gone and why. I want you to
explain to him why.

ANNE KATHERIN: Look I don't
want —

IRMA: If someone doesn't go down to
him, he'll just starve to death in
there. Eventually. He'll never come
out of his own accord. Here are
some cigarettes for him. Goodbye.

ANNE KATHERIN: You can't just go
like that. You can't just leave me.

IRMA: Why not, there's nothing else
to say, is there?